Over a long grave, in a quiet corner down by the river in Bangkok, is a covering of stone, grey and white, beautiful in the simplicity of its layered design. On it are engraved the names of all those whom the Lord called to himself on that sunny, carefree morning of 14 January 1978.

Ian Christopher Gordon-Smith	aged 37 years
Stephanie Joy Gordon-Smith	aged 30 years
Rachel Joy Gordon-Smith	aged 6 years
Mark James Gordon-Smith	aged 4 years
Lukas Juzi	aged 5 years
John Kennedy Farrington	aged 5 years
Iona (Twink) Paterson Parry	aged 31 years
Rebekah Linnet Parry	aged 5 years
Adèle Helen Parry	aged 2 years
Noel John Sampson	aged 31 years
Louise Ann Sampson	aged 30 years
Benjamin Richard Sampson	aged 2 years

Beside the names, in Thai and English, for all who will pass that way to read, are the words of Psalm 16:11 RSV –

**THOU DOST SHOW ME THE PATH OF LIFE;
IN THY PRESENCE THERE IS FULNESS OF JOY;
AT THY RIGHT HAND THERE ARE PLEASURES FOR
EVERMORE**

A permanent witness to the faith which drove them far from their homes in obedience to their Lord's command
to 'go',
to 'heal the sick',
and to 'make disciples of all'.

OMF International was founded by James Hudson Taylor in 1865 as the China Inland Mission. It now works in countries right along the Asia Pacific Rim. While evangelism and church planting are the Fellowship's central thrust, it also finds placements for Christian professionals with a wide range of expertise.

In His Time

IAN GORDON-SMITH

Compiled by Eileen L. Gordon-Smith, Ian's mother,
with deep gratitude for the prayers and encouragements of
his father, and always sensitive to what would be
approved by the Ian they knew so well

OMF International

CHRISTINA PRESS
CROWBOROUGH, EAST SUSSEX

Copyright © OMF International 1998
The right of Eileen L. Gordon-Smith to be identified
as the author of this work has been asserted by her in
accordance with the Copyright, Designs
and Patents Act 1988

First published in 1981 by Mrs Eileen L. Gordon-Smith
First OMF edition 1984.
This edition 1998.

British Library Cataloguing Data
A catalogue record for this book is available
from the British Library.

ISBN 1 901387 10 0

Designed and produced by Bookprint Creative Services
P.O. Box 827, BN21 3YJ, England for
CHRISTINA PRESS LTD
Highland House, Aviemore Road
Crowborough, East Sussex, TN6 1QX.
Printed in Great Britain.

Contents

Foreword

14 January 1978. In the previous four years, three OMF missionaries in Thailand had been murdered. Now a minibus had crashed: five missionaries from Manorom Christian Hospital were killed outright, together with seven children and three unborn babies.

I was speaking at a conference in Indonesia when I heard about the crash. We were taking a break in the middle of my two-part lecture on the humanity of Christ. A pastor handed me a copy of an Indonesian newspaper, and pointed to the front page. A report of the tragic death of twelve 'foreigners' in Thailand. 'Were they from your mission?' he asked.

There was no mistaking who they were. There were not two hospitals at Manorom. I was numb. Mystified. Questions would not go away. Why should these of all people be taken? Why should it happen at such a time? How could God let the carelessness of a truck driver bring about the loss of these young lives? It was with leaden feet and a heavy heart that I rose to continue my lecture. The second half of the discourse on the humanity of Christ, who bore our sufferings, assumed new relevance.

Why did this tragedy happen? Why do tragedies happen? How do we explain the inscrutable? To what purpose? When Job faced inexplicable tragedy, he did not try. He worshipped – he tore his clothes, shaved his head and fell to the ground. He realised there was no answer. But his faith was firm: 'The Lord gave and the Lord has taken away; may the name of the Lord be praised' (Job 1:20–21). Not 'why?' Not 'what for?' But a statement of faith. 'The Lord. . . .' The Lord who reigns. The Lord who is on the throne. The Lord who works all things together for his purpose. The Lord who acts in love in everything he does, even when we do not understand. Somehow, though Job didn't know how, the Lord was still in control.

When death strikes, our natural reaction is to ask, 'Why has the Lord taken?' Job went back to what he knew – the fundamental fact – 'The Lord gave.' He is the Lord who gives. He gave his only Son. He gave these young people. He allowed their lives to be a special witness and testimony to the people of Thailand. He has given us their story today. Twenty years on, we are challenged.

Then Job lays hold on a second fact. The Lord who gives is at the same time the Lord who takes. No matter how arbitrary the circumstances may seem, there are no accidents for God's children. He, the Lord, the one who numbers the very hairs on our heads, is the one who takes away. Nothing touches us apart from his will. And if something has been allowed to touch us then, as his children, we recognise that it has become his will for us. There we find an answer – for in his will is our peace; and that is where tears turn into life-giving water.

Paul wrote from his prison cell: 'I eagerly expect and hope . . . that now as always Christ will be exalted in my body, whether by life or by death' (Phil 1:20). There were no second causes in his life. He had but one goal for his ministry – to see that 'the greatness of Christ will shine out clearly in my person' (NEB). That was the ambition of those whose lives were taken twenty years ago.

This book tells something of their story. 'The Lord gave and the Lord has taken away; may the name of the Lord be praised.'

David W. Ellis
Sevenoaks
14 January 1998

My 'Reasonable Service'
(*Rom 12:1*, AV)

'Thanks a lot, Ian, it's been a beautiful morning,' said Noel Sampson, as the little hospital minibus neared Manorom on the highway in central Thailand.

'We're not home yet,' replied Ian, and within a few minutes he, with Noel and ten others, missionaries and their children, were home – with the Lord.

* * *

Ian's childhood was normal, happy and secure, except for the first four years of sleeping in air-raid shelters, and without the (unobtainable) delights of toys. He exhibited an enthusiasm for life in all its aspects, whether work, study, games or fun.

Ian's education had been planned from birth. His father was on the staff of Barclays Bank and this meant that there was an opportunity for a son to work for a special scholarship. Ian won this and at the age of thirteen passed into Haileybury College, Hertford. His first year there, particularly in the second term after Christmas, was so marred by homesickness that his parents wondered, briefly, if

11

they would be able to leave him there. A letter from him expresses his feelings at this time:

The homesickness has grown much worse this afternoon, and I am going quite crazy. I don't know how I can possibly stick another week and that's a fact. The sermon this morning was all about a boy's opportunities, particularly here. The trouble is the next holidays are only four weeks and then back for twelve more. Oh, it's terrible! It's like a nightmare. I pray for courage every day and for the homesickness to stop. [It did!]

During his early years, Ian had been taken regularly to church and had joined the local Crusader class. He learned to love the Lord and committed his life to him when quite young. He joined with enthusiasm in all that Crusader activity had to offer, whether Sunday Bible classes, indoor 'squashes', or 'wide games' in the park – he loved it all. During the spring and summer vacations of teenage years he went away to schoolboy camps, at Iwernminster and at Lymington; at the latter he developed a great interest in sailing. Those days of camp were also times when his spiritual life grew and deepened, and he began to have a hunger to do God's will, whatever that might entail.

Life at Haileybury became a settled pattern of steady work, growing friendships and much enjoyment, particularly after the 'fagging' era had passed! Ian took a great interest in all forms of sport, both as player and spectator. Though not excelling in any particular sporting activity, he played a good game of tennis and squash, swam and loved sailing. He played cricket at school, and was almost always to be found as a spectator at Lords on Gillette Cup Final Day. He remembered the thrill of other occasions at Lords – the Varsity match, and seeing David Sheppard make ninety plus for Cambridge, and Colin Cowdrey batting for Oxford against the pace bowling of Cuan McCarthy – and the style and elegance of others such as Ted Dexter, Rohan Kanhai and Clive Lloyd.

Ian was tremendously interested in Rugby football, whether playing in his house team, rooting for the 'Light Blues' at Twickenham, or watching his own school encountering another team. All were extremely important to him, though he learned eventually to get them in perspective. Years later on one dull and damp Saturday afternoon when he went over to watch Tonbridge School playing at home to Haileybury, there was a lull in the noisy support and his raised voice could be heard shouting encouragement to his own school. After the match, with Haileybury well beaten, he walked up the field to the rest of the family, and he said, 'Time was when *that* would have been an unmitigated disaster – now it's just a bother!'

Ian's interest in soccer crystallised into support for Manchester United, whose fortunes he followed for the rest of his days, particularly after having been deeply moved as a young man when disaster befell 'the Busby babes' at Munich, and half the team was killed as the plane crashed on take-off. Ian wrote of his deep distress at the loss of these fine young men, with the heart-cry: 'Turn back the clock and bring back yesteryear!'

It was during his last two terms at Haileybury that Ian started, seriously, to keep a diary, sometimes sitting late into the night expressing his feelings and recounting the day's events in great detail. Life at this stage was full of interest and anticipation. He studied hard, read widely and engaged in lengthy discussions with his contemporaries – again, often far into the night.

He hated change, however, and came to his last year at Haileybury with a certain amount of apprehension and sadness, as he thought of leaving friends with whom he'd worked and played for five years. On his eighteenth birthday he wrote:

> My birthday! Seventeen had seemed a long year, but now I reach the end of it I feel a constant nostalgia for things left behind. Even now I'm aware of events forgotten, and even despised at the time, which can never be recaptured. Memory cannot recall so much. That is why I feel I must write this – as an aid to memory. So as I pass from security to the reality of adult life in October, I'll remember seventeen as a happy year, one I hope to remember always, but is now gone and, sadly, can never be reclaimed.

Many years later, after a service in which the hymn 'Oh God our help in ages past' had been sung, he wrote:

> 'Oh God our help in ages past.' How this hymn used to revive me each day of a new term at school. Only five years there at Haileybury – sounded a long time then, but now only a fraction of my life. But an indelible fraction. A part given to learning and relearning. A wonderful time in reality.

So Ian left school, leaving behind his younger brother Bruce who had joined him for the final year. After much thought he had decided that he was called to a medical career, and having gained his first MB at school, he went on to Caius College, Cambridge, to read medicine. Here he was fortunate enough, during his first year in residence, to be able to share rooms with John Watson (later to become the Rev. John Watson), whom he had come to know through 'camp', and together they linked up with the CICCU (Cambridge Inter Collegiate Christian Union). Within its ranks Ian made true and lasting friends with whom he was in contact for the rest of his life.

He enjoyed Cambridge immensely – the challenge of learning theoretical and practical medicine, the friendships, the debates, and the spiritual growth of those years. For it was at this period of his life that he started recording in his diary the notes of his daily Bible study, and applying the teaching to his own life and problems. This habit continued through the years and became a blessing, not only to himself, but to many others. He also honestly recorded difficulties he found in Scripture:

Luke 16:20–31.
The story of Lazarus and Dives – a real problem. 'Is Hell eternal?' has been worrying me of late. Many say 'yes'. See Mk 9:43–48, etc. But can God tolerate eternal torment? Must he not step in and destroy? Is Satan never to be annihilated? Did God when he made the world with omniscience not realise the future damnation of some, and if so, why was his hand not restrained? These worry me. But there must be an answer beyond our ken. There must be more to this.

The blind man healed. Luke 18:41–42.
A simple request after earnest supplication: 'Lord that I may receive my sight.' Is that not the question all of us ask? Our sight, spiritually, needs to be lighted up. If it were, the doubt and fears would flee, the weak evangelism would be shown to be criminal, the weak prayer to be neglect of power and riches. All for the want of insight. Needed too in the physical realm – need insight to see the right things to touch, the things to leave alone, the places to visit and those to abhor. Blindness needs to be alleviated in every sphere – Jesus alone can do this.

I feel so weak as a Christian. A study of his word alone will keep me right with him. Yet this has for me always been the devil's strongest attacking point.

Luke 6:11–38.
Note 5:16. 'He withdrew to the wilderness and prayed.' 6:12. 'He went out into the hills to pray and all night he continued in prayer to God.'

What an amazing insight into the secret of Jesus' power. Not on the roadway was the battle won, but alone on the hillside. Not in the crowded streets, but in the wilderness. Never forget this, Ian. He who prays much has much power with God. Keep me prayerful, Lord.

The story of the miraculous draught.
Luke 5:1–11. 'At thy word we will.'
One verse: 'We toiled all night and caught nothing' (v. 5).
That's us. Working so hard often in our own energy for Jesus.
Seeking to catch men for the kingdom but so often catching
nothing.

Depression – lethargy in work and prayer – ineffective
ministry – vicious circle – Satan has won!

v. 5: 'At your word I will let down the nets.' That's the key.
At your word. It's his word that has power. His command to
be obeyed, his gospel to be preached. His call to be responded
to and his followers to be built up. Remember 'At thy word'.

Daniel 10:19.
The angel visits Daniel, 'greatly beloved'. What a man Daniel
must have been. Some title to have been given. Yet he feels
weak and sinful in the presence of this one who is so mighty.
Then encouraged and helped. So in Christian work. Feelings
of weakness and sin are the prerequisites for successful
calling upon God. Over-confidence in this field is a bad and
harmful trait. I must learn this.

Many opportunities for Christian work evolved. The
regular CICCU prayer meetings, participation in the missionary breakfast and leprosy prayer group; visiting
many 'freshers' to invite them to meetings, and the sub-
sequent joy of seeing some of them come to know the
Lord; increasing speaking engagements. All these, plus
more opportunities to enjoy sport, and the pleasure of
punting on the Cam led him to write: 'Time goes very
quickly with packed days.'

Ian was a very normal young man. He was attractive to,
and attracted by, the opposite sex, and if, in addition, they
were Christians, he was always on the look-out for the
one who would become his life partner. So when, at the
age of twenty, he became infatuated with a girl who was
not right for him, and who realised it herself, it was a

bitter experience, but all part of his spiritual pilgrimage. He had so entrusted the choosing of a wife to the Lord, that in all the years leading up to his meeting with Stephanie, he was never allowed to make a fatal mistake.

At the end of this brief friendship, he recorded in his diary:

> Tuesday 11 October, 1960 – A GREAT DAY.
> Today a letter from B. I went up to my room and read it, and it left me in no doubt of what was to happen. There was something definite about it that told me to say, 'No more!' After all, had I not asked God to stop me now or never? Had I not asked for his decision? And now it had come. At first, of course, it was a bitter blow. I suppose I'd known all along she's felt little for me, but I had trusted in our circumstances to bring us together. But it was not to be. The one redeeming feature was that I had not seen her for three months, really to meet, and now that God had said 'no' I knew it was for the best.

And two months later, after a diary gap:

> As I take up the story of the last two months or so of 1960, one factor predominates. That is the pre-eminence again of my spiritual life. During my second year I regret that I lapsed badly several times concerning my 'quiet times', and my desire to evangelise. I could not read Christian books comfortably. And I would put all this down to one fact, or one chiefly. The thought of B was becoming a destructive weapon in my life. I could not pray. I could not read a Christian book, because I constantly compared the experiences in it with hers, and found that so often she came pitifully short in her hunger for spiritual growth; and her affection for the world was too great. My whole spiritual life was running at a loss. I continually wanted to be away from Cambridge, as B was not here, so my time here seemed dull and lacking. Now, on this day I was free – free to forget, free to begin again. God had said 'no'. I could no longer hope it was his will – he said 'NO'. I had prayed in the Lake District that he would stop me

here – and he did. The first of many answers to prayer I was shortly to experience. The break was difficult at first. Going through it was very tough – it hurt. I burned several old mementoes and letters. I cleared away the traces, and endeavoured, gradually, to begin again. These things made the change easier. Steadily my interest was going, and I was forgetting. I found my love for the Lord growing day by day, and my zeal for him increased 100%. This operated in several spheres. First my own spiritual life – I passed through a time of untold blessing. God helped me to forget and made himself very real to me. In his presence was fullness of joy. Also I found further friends in Les, Peter Mulhall and others – the latter especially being a guide and help. My work became no longer a drag, but a pleasurable pastime. The leprosy prayer groups formed another outlet. I was now leader, and we had some grand times.

There were passing and superficial friendships in Ian's life during the next few years, but because of his determination to let God do the choosing, he was not allowed to get involved with the wrong partner.

Ian left Cambridge, but not the friends he made there. To three of these he was 'best man' at their wedding, his quick wit and easy manner making him ideally suited to this office, which he performed five times in all. Two of these friends, subsequently looking back to Cambridge days, spoke of Ian.

From Peter Mulhall: 'I have never had a friend whose friendship meant so much as Ian's; at Cambridge, down at Lymington camps, at Cheltenham while he was there, and many other places over twenty years. Fellowship with him was so happy, and so full of both fun and mutual encouragement.'

From Fred Heatley, at Caius College with Ian: 'For myself, as I think of my old friend Ian, I can but reflect that he lived his life as God meant him to, that he lived it well and he spent it well. Marvellous memories of those excit-

ing days in Caius flood into my mind, and Ian's delightful personality and cheerful good nature seem to banish
the present gloom: Ian's faith was always so fresh and so
exciting. He was always such a cheerful dynamic bundle
of energy. I don't think I can ever recall his being despon-
dent, at least not for longer than a minute! If there was a
sound of laughter round a corner you would expect to
come across Ian when you rounded it. I recall so clearly
his delightful and characteristic mirth when he discovered that Basil Atkinson had expounded for an hour and
a half from his battered Greek Bible, which he had been
holding upside down throughout the whole evening! Yes,
Ian was a delightful friend and marvellous companion.
His twinkling and lovely personality remain as a light to
inspire me as a fellow pilgrim.'

In November 1965 Ian spent a day in Cambridge with
Fred (now married), and afterwards wrote:

> Today I journey back, back to Cambridge with its colleges
> and spires, its streets with memories of a youth in its fullness,
> now five years past. Very sad to feel that so long separates the
> CICCU and Caius days from the present. I only wish we
> could live it all over again. I wasted so much time there and
> failed to utilise it fully. Now with Fred, Kath and child we
> revisited the former places, and punted up river as of old.
> May God satisfy my longing I pray. Life is too short!

From Cambridge, Ian entered the Middlesex Hospital,
and soon became immersed in his practical training, and
qualified MB, BChir (Cambridge) in July 1964, followed
by his MA in January 1965. Through these years of study,
he never forgot that God had the first place in his life.
Thus he sought to communicate his faith to patients as
opportunity arose. Letters from relatives show this. To
quote but one from the wife of a young man who was in
the Middlesex Hospital many weeks with a terminal
illness: 'Your were so kind to take John "under your

wing" and give him the spiritual knowledge and comfort he so desperately needed. You were well qualified and called to help him towards being a true Christian. In this way he was prepared, and died, and for this I shall always remember you with gratitude.'

Another one wrote after the death of her mother at the 'Middlesex': 'You cheered her up a lot by being a Christian and that made a tremendous difference to her – whether you knew it or not! For myself I want to thank you for a final smile and "wink"? That smile of yours reassured me through that night.'

Yet another relative, also appreciating the lighter side of Ian's character, sent with grateful thanks a very clever cartoon of Ian as a young House Surgeon, saying, 'I had an idea somehow that you like a bit of fun – with so many thanks for everything that you've done for Mother *and* me.'

Ian believed, as he put it, that 'patients are not "cases" but people with problems'.

Apart from work and study, during the latter half of his training he arranged and led regular meetings to encourage interest in OMF International (see p. ii). He became president of the hospital Christian Union, and when his time there was finished a letter on behalf of 'the Physios' said, 'For steady loyalty and work for him [open meetings, chapel services and houseparties] we thank you, Ian.'

19 March 1964 – twenty-fourth birthday:
When he the Spirit of Truth is come he will guide you into all truth: for he shall not speak of himself – but whatsoever he shall hear that shall he speak. My birthday verse – and how vital to me. In past weeks and months I have been amazed at the rapidity with which life is slipping away; twenty-five soon and then I'll really be getting on! But oh how I feel the need of a guide.

Ian worked hard, but never at any stage of his life took success for granted, as is shown by his diary entries over the days of his qualifying exams.

16 June 1964:
Finals begin. 'The fear of the Lord is the beginning of wisdom.' Go with me, Lord, today I pray – I feel so weak and unlearned but thou knowest far more than I. So provide for me I pray you today.

17 June 1964:
'Awake thou that sleepest.' Tricky yesterday. Overdid work Monday night and nearly fainted in exam, but God heard me and brought me through. Praise his name.

26 June 1964:
Late for viva today but he still with me guiding and helping. Ever the same Lord.

1 July – final morning of exams:
God helped me and I rejoice in him. At the beginning I knew he wanted me to pass. But had to work, and having done so I feel assured of success.

4 July 1964:
PASSED FINALS – Thanks be to the Lord Jesus who gives us the victory.

17 July 1964:
So thrilled today – such splendid news. Dr Ball's Houseman to be! All hurdles jumped – hallelujah! He's a wonderful Lord!

Immediately after passing his finals, Ian went to Uganda for an elective period of six weeks. His base was in Kampala, where Christian friends made him very welcome. He travelled a great deal during this time, getting lifts where he could to tour mission hospitals, helping where possible and learning something of medical work in a different culture. He wrote extensive daily diaries during this time, giving a vivid picture of life in this country which has since experienced such suffering.

On returning to the UK he took up his post as House Physician to Dr P.A.J. Ball at the Middlesex Hospital. Ian's vision was kept clear by regular study of God's word, something which he had mentioned earlier in a diary as essential to his Christian life, but which he didn't always find easy. As he started his 1965 diary he wrote on the opening page, 'SEARCH THE SCRIPTURES.'

BEGUN, 23 APRIL 1965:
'Wherewithal shall a young man cleanse his way – by *taking heed* according to thy word' (Ps 119:9).

Ian not only wrote about his blessings, his aspirations, his ideals, his promises to God, but also about his weaknesses and failures. The following extracts of diary entries through the years build up a picture of one who majored on obedience, constantly sought God's guidance, but being human, failed often. Most of his self-criticism seems to have been written following his daily Bible study.

I Cor 13.
These virtues are those which I so badly need as a doctor. I cut no ice for God. Why – because these qualities of life are missing. Annoyance, rudeness and irritability are all part of me. Patience, kindness, believing the best are qualities I covet, but in practice are often far behind. Lord, help me to be like you I pray.

Mt 18:22. Forgive – seventy times seven! What a strain that is but it must be done! I give in after two or three times.

How my pride needs to be crushed. Always so self-assertive!

Why is pride so terrible? Because it is a direct negation of God – of his power, his presence and his rule over us.

March 1964: John 12:43.
'They loved the praise of men more than the praise of God.'

My failing at the moment. This criticism could well be levelled at me. Oh that I might be more true, more out and out for him.

March 1965:
Ian, suppress your anxiety about house jobs. God has a life work for you to do and he will lead you step by step into it. . . . He has a life partner for you which he will reveal in his time.

December 1965:
O God, help me to obey you in all aspects –
   In my career
   In my finances
   In my wife
   In my future plans
   In my service
   In my living.

Ian, avoid gossip and titbits and passing on information re others. Lord, observe me here I pray.

I Cor 9:25. 'Every athlete uses self-control. So run to obtain the prize.' Lord, I pray for self-control in driving and in speaking. And for wisdom in judgement, and may I run to obtain *your* prize.

[When studying Job.]
He uses the seeming tragedy and disaster to bring about his purposes. 'Except a corn of wheat die. . . .' May I be prepared to face adversity.

Ian realised that victory in the Christian life depended very much on faithfulness in keeping his 'quiet time', and a few years later he wrote down his own rules concerning it.

1. QT must come first, i.e. before BBC news which distracts and diverts attention.
2. Early rise.
3. Failure here will *not* be corrected later in the day in 99% of instances.

4. Although this time is not the centre of Christian life, it is a
   barometer of its health and vigour.
He who is faithful in little is faithful also in much.

This must be my key. My Lord, you are the one my heart
loves. I adore you above all. Send me where you will. May
my life be spent for you.

All as yet unfixed, undecided, *uncharted* water for me.
What will happen? I affirm in all of these, 'I seek not mine
own will but the will of him that called me'. May he hold me
to this.

'Step forth upon the seeming void and feel the rock
beneath.' (Carmichael)

24 January 1965:
O may I serve God and my fellows –
to go the extra mile –
so important in medicine.

That service to God and his fellows in the field of medicine crystallised in the following appointments:

9.64 – 2.65	House Physician	Dr P.A. J. Ball
		The Middlesex Hospital
3.65 – 8.65	House Surgeon	Mr A. Elton
		Mount Vernon Hospital
9.65 – 2.66	House Surgeon	Mr W.R. Winterton,
		Mr K. Jackson and
		Mr R. Lloyd-Jones
		The Middlesex Hospital
4.66 – 9.66	Casualty SHO	Mr J. Shelswell
		Southend General
		Hospital
3.67 – 8.67	House Surgeon	Mr P.H. Newman,
		Mr D.R. Sweetman
		The Middlesex Hospital
9.67 – 5.68	SHO General Surgery	Mr L. Leask,
		Mr W. Bradfield

		Kingston General Hospital
5.68 – 12.69	Registrar General Surgery	Mr R. Harvey, Mr P. Boreham and Mr J. Fairgrieve Cheltenham General Hospital
1970 – 1971	Registrar General Surgery	Mr J. Lees Ferguson The Middlesex Hospital
1971 –1972	Clinical Assistant	Mr H. Thompson St Mark's Hospital
9.72 – 8.73	Surgeon at Manorom Christian Hospital, Central Thailand (on leave of absence from The Middlesex Hospital)	
1974 – 8.76	Senior Registrar – St Mary's Hospital, London	
8.76 – 1.78	Senior Surgeon at Manorom Christian Hospital, Central Thailand (on leave of absence from St Mary's Hospital)	

It was in 1969 that Ian obtained his FRCS. Just before the written paper, on 2 May 1969, he wrote:

Thou art my lamp, O Lord,
My God lightens my darkness.
By my God I can leap over a wall.
This God his way is perfect.
The promise of the Lord proves true.
He is a shield for all those who take refuge in him.
O Lord, go with me now I pray you. Equip me. Guide me into all truth and bring everything to my remembrance. May your will be done today.

True religion – pure – undefiled. Jas 1:27.
Lord, may I be used to relieve the afflictions of others. May my tongue and my life be pure I pray you.
Nowadays I make it a practice always to pray about tricky

cases. I need God's help in all things. So worried today re Mrs
C. A real problem. O Lord, help I pray you. I can do nothing
without you.

RESEARCH: As described by Ian and for which he was
eventually awarded his Master of Surgery (MChir,
Camb.).

My second year at The Middlesex Hospital was devoted to
full-time research into post-operative deep vein thrombosis
with particular reference to fibrinolytic activity of blood and
to prevention of thrombosis by subcutaneous heparin. An M
Chir thesis outline entitled 'The Incidence, Aetiology and
Prevention of Post-operative Deep Vein Thrombosis' has
been accepted by Cambridge University and this thesis is
now near completion.

Testimony to the value of this work is contained in tributes after he died from Ian's Chiefs: From Mr H.H.G.
Eastcott, Consultant Surgeon, St Mary's Hospital: 'Ian did
extensive research into the St Mary's Hospital series of
abdominal aortic aneurisms the year before he went to
Thailand; this work, involving computer analysis of
many aspects of the problem, certainly uncovered important evidence on the incidence and prevention of the most
important complication of the arterial graft operation for
this disease, namely infection of the graft. The importance
of preventive antibiotic treatment is clearly shown, I
believe for the first time, and many lives and much suffering will be saved when we publish.

'All of us on Zachary Cope ward loved and respected
Ian; there was a fine surgical future waiting for him on his
return.' (Thesis published October 1978)

Also from Mr H.H.G. Eastcott in St Mary's Hospital
magazine: 'St Mary's was fortunate to secure such a brilliant man and Ian was glad to come to us for his Senior
Registrarship. He soon showed his fine natural capabil-

ities as an operator, and was before long undertaking most of the major arterial reconstructive procedures on his own, with good results, all with a calm, modest assurance that drew admiration and respect from his peers and his chiefs alike.

'The sad mystery of his passing, and our grief at his loss must be balanced, at least in part, by the greatness of his character and his work, both of which will stand as a lasting memory and inspiration to us whom he leaves behind.'

Mr J.R. Kenyon, Consultant Surgeon: 'This is a loss to British surgery because Ian had a brilliant future, not only as a practising surgeon but in the teaching of his students. His moral integrity was an example to us all.'

Professor L.P. Le Quesne, DM, MCh, FRCS, Department of Surgical Studies, The Middlesex Hospital, London. In a letter to Ian's parents: 'I have such a clear and happy recollection of Ian during the period he worked in this department. Apart from his skilled and thoughtful care of his patients, it was during his time here that he carried out most of his splendid research work on deep vein thrombosis. I do hope you realise and take some comfort from the very real contributions he made to our surgical knowledge.

'These contributions remain with us, as do our very vivid memories of Ian himself, for as I write this it is not so much his professional attainments but his wonderful qualities as a man that are in my mind – his sincerity, his love of his family, his high ideals, his deep Christian faith, his real concern for the underprivileged people he went to serve. Few people gave so much to their fellow men in so tragically short a life as Ian.'

Professor Dudley, St Mary's Hospital, in an article in *The Lancet*: 'Ian Gordon-Smith was an energetic and skilled surgeon with a particular interest in vascular disease. Of outgoing personality and cheerful mien he was a pleasure to work with and able to draw the best from all those around him. Quite without affectation or personal ambition, he had endeared himself to all his colleagues at the Middlesex and St Mary's. His death at an early age is a great loss to British surgery.'

The 'Right' One

Throughout the years of hospital life and until he was twenty-eight years of age, Ian was constantly looking to the Lord to show him the life partner planned for him. He had certain standards from which he would not deviate. In 1965 he had written in his diary:

> It must go on record for me and before the Lord this day that 'as for me and my house we will serve the Lord', and I have no intention of being 'unequally yoked' [2 Cor 16:14–15, AV].
> If she is to be mine –
> Three things – 1. She must be converted.
>   2. She must love me.
>   3. She must be the right one.

On his twenty-fifth birthday:

> To me this is a major milestone. It signals perhaps the end of student-style days. The end of the Cambridge-Middlesex era. As I write, a lump in my throat is suppressed – the thought that the days of youth, golden days, are almost over – the freedom from care in Cambridge, the joyful friendships at Middlesex – these are gone, never to return. Marriage for some, careers for all, distance and ambition have taken over.

Relationships break, life rushes on. There is no time to ponder, to stay awhile. What now – today twenty-five? This age surely is for me the end of 'youth' in its fullest sense. I *must* be a *man* from now on and thirty cannot be far away. Ten years ago aged fifteen at Haileybury I thought of marriage and thought of its enjoyment – at earliest in ten years time! Well, here I am, still as much single as ever! I take Psalm 1 as my keyword for the next one, five even twenty-five years.

Ian never took the blessings of life for granted. On Christmas Day 1968, just before the very special year that was to follow, he wrote:

The blessings of Christmas here today. I have counted mine, my home, education, hospital jobs and all else. Too good for me. God is very merciful and kind. The infinite descended to the finite. And thus I believe that the infinite God can see and listen to my thanks for all his mercies to me today, not least his longsuffering, forgiveness and keeping power. I desire above all to follow his way and be like him.

CHELTENHAM 1969 – a lovely town, and a wonderful year for Ian, for it was here that he met Stephanie Baldock. Her home was in Ealing, she was educated at Notting Hill High School, and was at St Mary's College, Cheltenham, training to be a PE teacher, while Ian was a Surgical Registrar at the General Hospital. They found themselves at the same church, and worked together for a special evangelistic outreach between the colleges, and their friendship grew. On 11 March he wrote, 'As never before I feel sure this is *the* girl for me.'

Stephanie was the ideal partner for Ian. Though eight years younger than him, she was mature for her age, and possessed of the gift of wisdom and commonsense which made her the sort of person to whom those much older than herself would feel they could turn for advice. This was to be a great blessing on the mission field later on.

Like Ian, she had a deep desire to seek God's will for her life, and to be obedient to it. And in the area of sport she was as interested as he. They both loved music, and with similar church and Crusader backgrounds, had much in common.

My twenty-ninth birthday. Greeted by birthday present from Stephanie with a card saying 'I love you'. No other present in this world could have been so wonderful as that. It is the Lord's doing. Today 1 Samuel 12:16 – 'Stand still and see this great thing which the Lord will do . . . Is it not wheat harvest?'

20 March – Ian proposed to Stephanie:

I plucked up courage. Do you think it's right? I think so, she said. Well then? You must give me time, she said. How long? I asked – how long? She paused – then just said, 'I love you, Ian.' I moved on – 'Well, will you marry me?' 'Yes, I will,' she murmured. Simple as that! Yes, but God has done it all. We talked of engagement, the ring, of friends, asking her father, her job. 'I'll make a hopeless wife,' she said. *Daily Light* and prayed together thanking God.

The verse tonight – 'Not one thing hath failed of all the good things your God said concerning you. All are come to pass unto you. Amen.' Praise him. Lord, may I never forget you.

4 April 1969:

God, my Lord, you are wonderful to prepare such a one as this for me. Perfect in every way she is.

Easter Day 1969 – John 20:19, 21, 26 – Peace be with you.
Lord who has safely brought me to the beginning of this day – thank you.
Thank you for my work.
Thank you for my family and friends.
Thank you for my school, college, hospital.
Thank you for this lovely day.

Thank you for my car.

Thank you for my darling who today becomes my fiancée in thy plan.

Thank you for Jesus above all.

28 November 1969, Cheltenham. At the end of a happy year Ian wrote:

> My last morning in Cheltenham. I have greatly enjoyed my time here. Stephanie, the excellent job, new friends, the town and prom, the Cotswolds – all these are a part of me. It has been a quiet, peaceful interlude – a stage of training on the road, the final two years of my twenties. Of achievement, maturity, surgical skill and qualification, and a more determined Christian walk. But of failure – yes. A failure to love, to seek and save those who are lost. God give me passion for souls and use me I pray you.

A short while before her marriage, Stephanie wrote in a letter to Ian: 'There seems nothing more wonderful to me than the thought of a lifetime spent with you.'

Ian and Stephanie were married on 27 December 1969. The night before, Ian's diary entry read:

> My last day a single man. Only twelve hours to go as I write. How wonderfully God has led us. S and I are so confident we are for each other. How super it all is. Here today at flat making up bed and we even laid our hearts open on sex and discussed it fully. Now I'm alone. V. much in love. Never more sure of my love. How fast it's gone. It seemed to DRAG but here it is. O Lord, be all in all to us please.

GORDON-SMITH – BALDOCK. On 27 December 1969, at Duke Street Baptist Church, Richmond, Ian Christopher, son of Mr and Mrs S. Gordon-Smith of Thundersley, Essex, to Stephanie Joy, daughter of Mr and Mrs J.A. Baldock of Ealing.

After a very happy honeymoon at the Old England Hotel, Bowness-on-Windermere, Ian and Stephanie settled in a flat in Ealing, Ian going daily to the Middlesex

Hospital, and Stephanie teaching PE at Southall Grammar School. Three months after marriage, Ian arrived at his thirtieth birthday, and recorded:

> Not a day that I had hoped would come! Now it seems that real youth is over. Sport is not now an objective – my rugger boots have been hung up for keeps probably, sadly. But what remains? Family life is just developing, and so is my opportunity as a speaker for Jesus. Never before have doors been so open. I long to use them for him. The miracle of the loaves and fishes (Mt 14:13) is so appropriate. But before our gifts can be used they have to be (1) in his hands, (2) broken at his will. Lord, lead me and my wife as you will I pray. Guide this year over Christian service, family, my MS or MChir. Show the way re work overseas, and make me into the man you want me to be.

They both had a responsible attitude towards the stewardship of their money.

21 August 1970:

> We have been thinking re our giving recently, and we are resolved to give 10% of our income after tax. This *is* a sacrifice this year. So it should be.

The marriage, though only lasting eight years, was very happy. On their first wedding anniversary, Ian wrote on his card to Stephanie: 'With all my love after a wonderfully happy year,' and shortly before his death he recorded: 'Our relationship has never been better.'

Just Rachel

On 22 May 1971, Stephanie's first baby, Rachel Joy was born. Ian was present at the birth, and wrote of that day in his characteristically forthright manner:

> Born 12.03 am. For me not a great experience I did not think. Possibly it was the forceps and the mass of people there. The baby did not look at all superb – blue and a squint! But a big cry and all was OK – no defect, which was a relief. I confess I was fed up it was a girl, but this I gather is the sentiment of many men. Heffie very tired.

Rachel Joy became a great joy in more than name, as a diary entry reveals on Ian's next birthday, when she was ten months old:

> 19 March 1972:
> Horrors! to wake thirty-two really comes as a shock. First birthday with Rachel Joy here too! She really is lovely.

And, on 27 March 1974, when she was two years and ten months:

> Lovely evening with Rachel. Had supper with us. I read to her and her goodnight prayer was:

Thank you for Neil and Richard.
Thank you for lawnmower for Daddy's birthday.
Thank you for Nana's birthday.
Thank you for Nana, gone away back on Saturday.
Thank you for, bye bye, Amen.
Adorable.

God's Call to Manorom

Though married life for Ian and Stephanie was so full and so happy, with work, Christian activities, many friends, and the giving and receiving of much hospitality, they still had an unanswered question in their minds: does the Lord want us here or overseas?

In 1971, while seeking to discern God's will in their lives, they 'chanced' to see an advertisement in the OMF magazine *East Asia's Millions*: 'Wanted – a surgeon – for one year at Manorom Hospital, central Thailand.' Both felt that this was a call to them, but prayed a lot and sought God's approval before making a decision to volunteer. This, they felt, was given. Ian's Professor at the Middlesex Hospital was at first reluctant to give Ian the necessary leave of absence, but subsequently did so, and preparations began to be made.

In March 1972 Ian recorded in his diary:

How busy life is. Seems little chance of being ready for Thailand in just six months – only five and a half in fact, but that's what I aim for. God must needs help me. Then Thailand! Next year I'll write this in very different circumstances, and in very different outlook, and at thirty-four? Ah, here's the crunch – here's the crucial question. May God guide me along his path to the place of his choosing all the way. Not my will but thine be done.

As the time drew near for the family's departure it was not without some apprehension that Ian recorded in his diary:

My mind is turbulent when I really think of it.

1. Thesis not finished
2. No language
3. No tropical medicine
4. Heat
5. Flies, rats, snakes
6. Lack real power.

Lord, these are my needs and more – for Rachel especially and journey, and Stephanie, May Ex 33:14 be sufficient for all – 'I will go with you in person and set your mind at rest.'

In September 1972 Ian and Stephanie, with Rachel, flew to Bangkok, and travelled on by bus about 120 kms to the small, well-equipped hospital set among the paddy fields of central Thailand. Within half an hour of arriving Ian was called upon to operate on a patient.

This year proved to be a rewarding experience, in spite of the initial difficulties of adjusting to the different food, climate, creatures, and bouts of malaria, which were particularly troublesome for Ian. Also there was the frustration of not having the language. This, however, proved an irresistible challenge, and by the end of the year Ian was able to interview most patients without an interpreter.

19 March 1973:
This year going so fast but one of my best years. Lord, use me in the years to come. May I be more diligent to see your will and to do it. More determined to live for you. May I obey all your guidance and direction, and never let me reject your clear voice.

And in July of that year:

> Today I prayed and committed the future to the Lord. We must let him have full disposal of us whatever he wants – Middlesex Hospital or here. Lord, in your hands. We want only the best. Please lead.

It was with very mixed feelings that the family returned to the UK in August 1973, as is shown by Ian's moving and prophetic diary entry for their last day at Manorom:

> Late last night I walked round the hospital and asked God to guide me back if his will to be done. I'd love it in one way and hate it in others. There's so much to feel that one could achieve, and to be serving the Lord here would be a source of joy and peace. But would it satisfy? Anyway I'm certain he will guide. And if it's here, I'm willing to BURY [his capitals] myself here. With this in mind we left Manorom after dawn at 6 am.

It took Ian and Stephanie some time to settle back into life in England. They missed the fellowship and work at Manorom, and they were shocked by the materialism they found in the West after their simpler life in Thailand. Two diary entries some months later recorded Ian's feelings about this:

> When we see this world's empty glory we realise how pointless it all is and how precious is real faith.
> Good to have the Hi-Fi on display. But I hold it lightly. Materialism in this life a curse.
> 'Only one life – 'twill soon be past – only what's done for Jesus will last.' Not for Professor, not for family, not for me. For Jesus.

15 October 1973:
> Rejoice always. Pray constantly. Give thanks in all circumstances. Why? This is the *will of God* concerning you. Want to know God's will? Here it is!

Ian returned to the Middlesex Hospital to finish his time as Surgical Registrar, and started to apply for Senior Registrar jobs. He didn't find it easy to achieve this, partly because of the measure of competition for such appointments, and also because he had been out of the country for a year. Early in 1974, after having been short-listed but failing to obtain several jobs, he and Stephanie decided that if by the end of January 1974 there was still no certain prospect, they would take it God wanted them back in Thailand, and back they would go! However, a few days before the day of decision, Ian was appointed a Senior Registrar at St Mary's Hospital, Paddington.

During Ian's time of uncertainty about future plans, Mark James had been born – on 26 October 1973. This event brought great joy to his parents, and Ian commented in his diary: 'Nice to have a baby boy to come home to!'

19 March 1974:
Thirty-four today! I liked Bruce's card – 'I didn't forget your birthday, but I will forget how old you are.' It's catching me up. Middle age approaches! I must use the time – what time there may be – for God.

The Vital Decision

For Ian and Stephanie, Thailand remained in the shadow of their lives, constantly being brought to mind as news of the hospital there came to them by letter, and through visits of missionaries as they came on furlough. At the end of December 1973 Ian wrote:

What of 1974? I pray God to guide my life and Stephanie's and show us his perfect plan. Does Thailand recede into the past – an isolated incident, or come back from the past again?

19 March 1974:
I feel a tremendous yearning for Thailand still. It's not possible to separate the feeling of desire to return to the land from the great sense of job satisfaction I had there. Certainly I'd love to do another year there. Really would! Maybe I can go but it's up to the Lord to decide.

30 March 1974:
So another day. And having begun my QT by glancing at negs of Thailand, I am still in mind to return. Of course now it's easy to overlook all the things we disliked, the heat, the snakes, the insects, the burglars, the food sometimes, the lack of freedom of movement. Those and much else forgotten, but

I still yearn for 'active' front-line service again – though we are all front line in a sense.

Early in 1974 Ian started his work as Senior Surgical Registrar at St Mary's. He carried on with his important thesis on deep vein thrombosis, which, with all his other commitments, was very time consuming, as he noted on 7 June:

Actually got on well with thesis. Great! Seem never to have time. Rush! Rush! Rush!

By the time this work was completed, Ian was well on the way to becoming a Consultant Surgeon – so why did he and Stephanie, with their two children, uproot themselves and return for a further period of service in Thailand? To answer this question, one must listen to their words at their valedictory service:

Ian:

I think there are two prerequisites to learning God's will for our lives. The first undoubtedly is a willingness to obey it when he reveals it. The wonderful thing about our previous year in Thailand was that, while we were there, we were absolutely conscious that this was the place that God wanted us to be. We never had a moment's doubt, and this gave impetus and drive to everything that we did – in fact, it made every single thing we did count. And the thing we learnt, I think, on return, was that this was the attitude that we'd got to adopt; that we'd got to be willing to obey God's will, whatever it was, when he revealed it.

The problem was then a correct discerning of the signs as he revealed his will to us, and this was never more true than in a case of short-term service in Thailand. For years now, the advertisements have been going out: for two or three years – 'Doctors, surgeons, nurses, physiotherapists, urgently wanted in Thailand'; and then underneath, in big black type: 'Long term only – some knowledge of the Thai language essential.' So there's no place for short-termers in Thailand today, the immigration, the visa situation, is so tight that the Mission just cannot afford to have to go through all the difficulties of getting someone in just for a year or two. And yet that's what we felt called to offer again. Moreover, as we were thinking about it, we knew that there were missionaries who were on the mission field, some short-term, but one or two long-term, who should never be there – they're misfits. Then you have others who, we're quite sure, ought to have been there, but weren't for some reason. And so we wanted to be absolutely certain of God's will as he revealed it to us. I think it came to us in four ways:

The first was a conviction, an inner conviction, that dawned over one or two years, that really our role in Thailand had not been played out, that God still had something for us to do, that we'd contributed something when we were last there. And this inward conviction that we still had a contribution to make grew over the first two years after we'd returned.

Added to this was the reception of the 'world'. By the 'world' I mean those in authority who had the ability to control where I would go next in my work, and who held the permission for me to leave this country again on leave of absence. They were, particularly, a chairman of the selection committee who was responsible for the rotation of surgeons and doctors in trainee posts; also, the Professor himself at the head of the pyramid, who understood the problems involved of people going abroad, leaving the trainee ladder, and then re-entering it, and who himself had to juggle with the pieces to fit a training rotation. To my surprise, when I first knew him (this was after I returned from Thailand), he was absolutely dead against my returning there; the only place he would countenance was the United States. Then one day he suddenly said, 'I see there's an advertisement for a surgeon in Nigeria. Do you want to apply for it?' My reply was, 'Well, if I were to go abroad anywhere at this stage, I would rather go somewhere where I know the culture and something of the language.' Strangely, starting with this advertisement about Nigeria, he changed his mind such that, a while back, he said to me, 'I don't mind for how long you go – I'm prepared to underwrite it for you.'

So there is the inward conviction and this favourable reception. Then there was the Christian discussion with those we knew well. Christians whom we could rely upon, whose judgement was sound. There were the Christians first of all, who were out there at the Mission hospital already. I wouldn't describe their judgement as unsound; I would describe it as slightly biased. A surgeon who is working under stress is only too ready to have the offer of someone else to work alongside him, and I wasn't very surprised, when I wrote to John Townsend and offered to come back and give two or three years' further service, when he jumped at the idea, and he said, 'Yes, for my part, I'd be delighted to have you back.' We'd got on very well the first time, and we could work together again – we knew that.

More important was the opinion of people who knew Thailand and who knew the hospital, but who weren't medical, and weren't going back to work there. We spoke to those folk, and, after two to three days thinking about it, they came back with the response, 'Yes, we do believe that this would be great; we believe that the Lord could really use you again in this way.' So Christian discussion favoured our return.

Then, finally, the combination of circumstances. First of all, our going back would fill a very real need. Just at this time of my career, when I would normally be leaving a part of the rotation to move on to another hospital, there would be a natural hiatus, and there is a hiatus in the surgical services at Manorom. Indeed, I think it's fair to say that since I was there, there hasn't really been a full-time surgeon in operation. John Townsend has had to do much of the surgical work part time, fitting it in with his administrative duties. Those latter duties are going to increase enormously when Ulrich Juzi, who's been sharing them with him, goes on furlough in November of this year. John's going to have to do much more administration. So I'm going to be able to go in, and take much of the surgical load from off his shoulders. Then the

second year that I'm there John himself is going to be on furlough, and I'm going to be able to cover for him when Ulrich
returns to take over the administration. During that second
year, for the last six months of it, a long-term surgeon, a chap
who has dedicated his life to work in that part of the world,
is going to arrive, and we shall be able to work together for
perhaps six months, seeing him into the job. So the timing is
absolutely right.

Then there's the remarkable incidence of the visa, or work
permit. One dentist who went out to work in Thailand spent
eleven months waiting for a work permit, was only there for
a year, and he was really only able to work for one month on
his own. We happened to be in Thailand in 1973, in a twelve-
week period when work permits were issued for the first
time, and during that twelve-week period they were issued
for life. If we'd left before that time, then we wouldn't have
any work permit. If we'd been there, and had been given our
work permits after that time, then they would have had a
completion date of a month or perhaps a quarter. But ours
were issued for life.

And so these four factors, the inward conviction, the
favourable reception, the discussion with Christians, and the
combination of circumstances, led us to feel that God has
revealed his will unmistakably for us to go back. This God-
given guidance was essential before we could undertake a
God-given task.

The work I'm going to do is specialised. It's a work which
requires training and experience, and that is, I believe, what
my main contribution is going to be. I haven't the understanding – the deep understanding of the culture, the handling of the language, to be able to go out and do
straightforward evangelism. I'm going to do medical work,
and I can add a little bit to what the pastor said in his prayer
about God having one Son and he being a missionary. He certainly was a missionary, and he healed – and when he healed
people, he didn't just heal in order that they might become
his followers. He healed because he loved them; he showed
compassion, and he showed God's love for its own sake to

these people. I believe that's what the medical work does – it goes hand in hand with evangelism, but it isn't merely the bait on the end of the hook. It is a part, a way, by which we show God's love for its own sake to people in desperate need.

It's a God-given task, and for it we're going to need God-given strength. Missionaries are not extraordinary people, that's absolutely clear. But I believe they are in an unusual situation. They face the very special pressures of a community which is alien to them in culture, in language, in habits, in diet and in climate, and, what's more, it's a closed community. There are enormous pressures – pressures of the emotions – because of the close nature in which people of different personalities live, and they become very stressful pressures at times. There are times when these pressures almost seek to get an outlet in explosive utterances. I remember one rather amusing instance when I was doing a ward round one day with one missionary nurse. Another one came up and started to complain about something which had been done incorrectly in her view, and she 'let her hair down' verbally for a moment or two, and then stumped off in a huff. The nurse I was with turned to me and said, 'She's a pain in the neck.' Quite spontaneously, because I felt this comment was discordant, I said, 'I don't really think that you ought to say that about your fellow missionary; you may feel it, but you ought to keep it to yourself. Comments made like that in theatre breed bitterness.' She didn't reply, but a few moments later perhaps five minutes, she turned to me and said, 'You know, you're quite right in what you said just now. I shouldn't have made that comment, but she *is* a pain in the neck all the same!'

There are these enormous emotional pressures which build up, and seek an outlet. Then there are pressures on one's physique. When I was there, I was absolutely astonished at the number of fit, tough, missionary people of young age who were continually going down, and being almost carried on a stretcher to hospital with some sort of undiagnosed fever. Working in this strange climate, in the humidity and the heat, was a real drain on one's physical energy; and it means that every time someone goes down it throws an extra load on the next person.

Then there's the pressure on one spiritually. Do we find it easy in this country to make time to pray? Do we find it easy to get up early, to read our Bibles? Do we find it easy to walk closely with the Lord? Well, believe me, it's just as hard on the mission field, and in a closed, tightly-knit Christian community it's just as difficult to pray and to get alone with the Lord. I remember sometimes in the evening I would see one missionary alone, walking out among the rice fields, and choosing a spot to sit down to read her Bible and pray, making time to get alone with God, because, without God-given strength for the task, then it becomes impossible. So there's God-given guidance for the God-given task, requiring God-given strength. What should be the Christian response?

I believe perhaps two. The first is the response of contact. We found it a most wonderful experience, the number of people, when we were out there last time, whom we got to know by letter – folk perhaps whom we, I'm afraid to say, never really got to know well on a personal basis in the church. We knew them by face, of course, but really we weren't quite sure that we could put a name to the face very often, and often we hadn't even so much as shaken hands with them. Yet they contacted us, and wrote to us, and this is a real lifeline. One is cut off in an area where one's only link with the outside world is radio, and people who come through from time to time, and the post day by day – something which people in that environment really look forward to. Letters from home, bringing news, bringing items of interest, for keeping one in touch with one's background – the lifeline, the post, the contact.

The second response, which we found enormously valuable last time of course, was prayer. Satan goes into a situation when one's doing work, not possibly in the direct attack, not in diverting one into saying, 'Well, I'm not going to bother to go and operate today because I don't feel like it'; not in just being bolshy and difficult; but, when one is tired and it's hot, and you've just two more patients to see, and they're being very tedious, the temptation is to lash out with the tongue, and to accuse them of being difficult and stupid, just to say something which others will hear, and it will set the whole Christian work back a month or two, and will get that doctor a bad name. Or, alternatively, to make some totally inexperienced mistake, a slip, a cultural slip, which will again cause offence.

Your prayers, prayers going up for us, perhaps in moments when we haven't had time to pray, perhaps in moments when we've been particularly under attack or under pressure, your prayers can support us and prevent those mistakes which could hinder God's work. So I leave you with this verse, from 2 Thessalonians, chapter 3 [RSV]: 'Finally brethren, pray for us, that the word of the Lord may speed on and triumph, as it does among you.'

And Stephanie:

Once we're there, what am I going to do? It's obvious what Ian's going to do – he's the surgeon. We've been very surprised, on two or three occasions, when people have turned to me and said, 'Are you going back as well, or is Ian going alone?' Well, this has been a great surprise to me; I wouldn't dream of letting him go off, I must say! But, apart from that, I think it does suggest that there is a role for a missionary wife abroad when she is obviously tied to the children. And so I want to tell you some of the things that I shall be aiming to do while I'm out there.

I think the very first thing is to provide a stable home life, so that Ian can be free to get on with his work energetically and efficiently. Obviously the stresses on the mission field can be quite great, and I think that, for single people, men and women, the stresses can be greater when they haven't got a particular person to turn to and confide in. So my first role will be just to provide a stable family home. Secondly, I hope to be a companion to others – the nurses who are already there, and also to the missionary mothers who are out there already, as a friend to listen, to talk to, to share problems with. I hope that I'll be useful in this field.

The third thing I shall be doing is quite a lot of baby-sitting during the day time, so that the other missionary mothers will be free to do language study or to use their language; and to free them from looking after their children so that they can do the missionary work which they are out there to do.

And fourthly, of course, to look after Rachel and Mark, who are five, and nearly three, and to teach them. And possibly to do some specific teaching with some of the other young children that are there, before they go off to their boarding school. So that's the role that I hope I'll be able to fulfil, and we will be very much relying on your prayers to help us. Thank you very much.

Medical Missionary – Reality

On 20 September 1976, once more Ian and Stephanie flew out, this time with two children. Ian's diary entry for that day records: 'Our last day at "137" before leaving. Wonder, strangely, if I'll see it again. Stupid really, as no reason to feel worried.'

The family didn't go immediately to Thailand. They flew first to Malaysia, in order to visit Chefoo School for missionaries' children, where it was possible that Rachel might have a couple of terms. They spent a short holiday in the lovely country and climate of the Cameron Highlands, and both Rachel and her parents were much impressed with what they saw of the school, set high up on the edge of the jungle, and approached by taxi up a steep, winding road.

This break was followed by a couple of weeks' language study in Bangkok, an uncomfortable experience owing to the heat, the noise and inadequate water supplies in the house where they were staying. So they were not sorry to find themselves at last on the tour bus to Manorom once more.

From the time of their arrival at the hospital, Ian and

Stephanie wrote to their families every week. Ian's first letter was encouraging. He wrote:

> Our start here has been amazing. Last time '72 you recall it was half an hour before I was called to see a patient. This time John rang me in ten minutes and guess what – it was a damaged artery behind the knee and I had to graft it – straight from Mr Eastcott's training! It seemed to set a seal on my arrival. They've not done such a case in living memory. The chap's leg was dead but today is alive and hot.

As so often happens in the Christian life, this seal of God's leading was followed by Satanic attack, and a month later Ian's letter said:

> Tuesday OPD [Out Patients' Department] was awful: not medicine, not surgery, not even GP – but farming! A proverbial cattle market. And then I was No. 1 Dr on emergency for all types from 5 pm Monday until 5 pm Tuesday, and, what with one thing and another, I felt like quitting and coming back – resentful and bitter that my training and hardly-acquired skills should be useless and likely to evaporate in time in this environment. I never felt like this all the year last time. Of course there's no novelty now, and the work in OPD is even less inviting. However, with your prayers and confidence this week I think I have come to terms with it, and have a peaceful and relaxed attitude to it. The medical patients I've admitted have all done well. The surgery has been successful with a good spirit in the operating room. The conference helped of course. All central Thailand plus Bangkok missionaries arrived, and for four days we've had great fellowship. The morning meetings by Dan Bacon really jolted me into the realisation that the medical work, etc. was 'for the Lord', and moreover, if this was God's will being fulfilled, no detriment to training or experience could possibly ensue.

Ian was already beginning to experience the difficulties which he had foreseen, and of which he had spoken at the valedictory service. In February 1977 a diary entry read:

Because others are away at this time, John and I are going to carry the surgical load. I don't mind doing it, but it is such *hard* work, working all the day and then having to do this big ward round in the evening, with many problems accruing, inevitably, to a large ward round. Also I've not really had much time to get on with the exam work (to be accepted for medical work in Thailand). Here we are – I've got clinical tropical diseases in front of me, and I really haven't got down to it yet. Nevertheless I'm doing my best; I don't think I'm being lazy, and I'm sure the Lord is going to put me right on this. I do feel, however, that I'm not giving him the rightful place in terms of 'quiet time'. It's almost ten days now since I had anything like a 'quiet time'. Just occasional moments of prayer to him. Most times I speak to him of course, but there's really been no sustained communication now for ten days. Although I'm really 'in the spirit' at meetings, I'm not having this personal contact. I must take note of Maurice Wood's rebuke in a Keswick address – I was listening to it on a tape last night – 'Christians on their way to heaven should be in bed before eleven. Most spiritual battles are won before 8 am.' Lord, help me to win this one I pray you. I'm very anxious, as this is a crucial point in my life, a time when, though not old, I'm no longer in the full flush of youth. I'm in my full strength now, and this is a time when I should be exerting myself for God; a time when I should, in a sense, be pulling out all the stops for him; a time to throw off childish thoughts and mannerisms and behaviour – to throw off shyness and reticence, and to become the sort of person God wants me to be. I must also throw off, to a certain extent, something of my reluctance over the Thai 'speaking' here.

Letter from Stephanie, 31 December 1976: 'The trouble is that other folk are working at the limits of their knowledge whereas Ian isn't. So some are frustrated because they feel pressurised and Ian is frustrated because he has to drop his (St Mary's Hospital) standards. He copes very well with it though, but I feel for him so much at times.'

19 March 1977: Ian said that this had been one of the happiest birthdays of his life. Presents in the morning, twenty of them, a trip over the river to Uthai later, and shopping in the market. Then back to a Christmas-type dinner, superbly cooked by Steph. In the afternoon the Parrys and the Farringtons and the Townsends gathered under the house for tea and birthday cake, and in the evening a delicious meal at the Farringtons. Ian says the emphasis on food is because such occasions are rare. Then a late-night listening to a football match, in which Manchester United scored a goal so exciting that Ian woke Steph up to tell her about it – but she forgave him!

There were many happy and refreshing interludes in that busy year of 1977. There were numerous visits to Bangkok, mostly for immigration purposes, when the family would meet up with their friends the Pickards, visits to the British Club, where seven free passes had been made available to OMF missionaries and where one could have a superb swim. Also, for Ian, a game of squash with Hanmer Webb-Peploe, who was working in Bangkok for the Shell Oil company. Ian had known Hanmer from Cambridge days, and he and his wife showed the family great kindness and hospitality on several occasions. There was also the excitement of shopping in Bangkok – a visit to 'Motif' in Silom Street, where beautiful materials could be obtained, and dresses made up very cheaply. Every trip to Bangkok would also include a visit to 'Central', the big department store, where, when funds allowed, 'goodies' unobtainable at Manorom could be bought.

There were picnics by the river, opportunities to take photographs of various colourful Thai festivals, and, best of all, holiday breaks, either in the OMF holiday house at Hua Hin, with its quiet beach, warm sea bathing and golden sands, or away up in the north of the country, above Chiang Mai, in Pinecrest, another OMF holiday house, a lovely log-cabin-type house set high up above the town among the trees. Here one could be cool, wear sweaters, and sit round a blazing log fire in the evening – this was Ian's favourite retreat. When possible, Sue and David Pickard (later to become the General Director of OMF International) with their three children, would join up with Ian and family for holidays. On one occasion, in June, when they were all at Pinecrest together, Ian wrote of an occasion when they set out to visit a lone OMF missionary in a remote tribal village:

It really was a superb spot on Doog Withanon, 8,500 feet, the highest mountain in Thailand. We went up via some superb waterfalls with notices 'Very dangerous. Several people have died here already!' Up some fifteen miles into the hills some 4,000 feet and OMF worker Leona Bair's village. She in Meo costume and a little straw-roofed hut. The fire in the centre of the floor on which we fried pork slices, the Meo in their 'costume' wandering in and out, and I had to examine two with illnesses and give an opinion. In the evening one brought a whole basket of corncobs as a present. In the afternoon we showered in a waterfall coming 500 feet down the precipice, so sheer that the water fell directly on you, and it was hard to stand up and bitingly cold. I held Mark in a small side one, much to his delight. That evening, all ate round the hut fire singing choruses, and the house slowly filled with Meo Christians coming to join and share items for prayer, e.g. – 'We buried some money and can't remember where. Now we need it again!' or 'Help us to find a lost pig.' Everyone prayed – some in English, some in Thai, and some in Meo. Bed at 10.15 on uneven earth floor with quilts underneath, in full clothing and cardigans. Colder than Pinecrest – probably 5,000 feet nearly. It had been a wonderful twenty-four hours.

I went to church on Sunday morning, and enjoyed very much hearing Samuel preach on 'the life that I now live' – the life of Christ that now lives in me, not the old life that can be taught to be better, but a completely new life. Not my life either, the life of Christ living in me – the life that wins.

March 1977:

Who knows what's going to happen in this next year? So many books we brought out to read, medical books, two volumes of Winston Churchill, Cromwell – all waiting to be read. Perhaps it is that this time I'm, maybe, a bit older, maybe feeling more tired; we don't *seem* to be doing so much as last time, but that may be a total fallacy. Certainly I'm doing far more effective surgery than I was last time. So we look forward to this year. Thirty-seven is getting away now from twenties. When you're thirty-six – well, you're close to thirty-five, which is mid thirties and doesn't seem very far away from the twenties. But thirty-seven, then thirty-eight – well, then it's forty, which seems to be the horror year. Well I can't say I'm horrified at the prospect, but I certainly will be quite happy to make the most of these next few years.

As the cool season passed, and the temperatures rose, the difficulties of missionary life became more apparent, and in April Ian wrote: 'The hot season is taking its toll a bit and it's very easy to get dehydrated and fed up. The extra mile must be travelled by many of us, but in what mood do we travel it?' He wrote to his parents: 'At this hospital we are trying to do the best in medical work plus the best in evangelism. In many mission hospitals you get one or the other – here we are trying to do both.'

During this month of April 1977, Andre Van Rij, a surgeon from New Zealand, stayed at Manorom for one month. A year later he wrote: 'Of more recent weeks I keep coming across work that Ian Gordon-Smith produced. He certainly was a fine and capable fellow, and his commitment to Manorom must certainly have been an enigma to his colleagues – and more so now. I really praise the Lord for the example of Ian, as I think upon it, even now while I write.'

May 1977, in a letter home, Ian wrote:

My chief problem is dealing with patients with too little cash to stay the course, who therefore take their discharge early and waste all the money they've spent. This is stressful, as every complication, e.g. failed skin graft, redeemable in UK, may be a total disaster here, and not *everything* works first time! Secondly, the need for good relationships among staff, especially with the OMF nurses in theatre. Usually no problem, but little things can be big in this close environment with few safety valves.

And in a later letter:

Tomorrow I'm leading the English service here, and I'm taking more from Hudson Taylor's biography. I'm now one third way through vol. 2 and finding a lot to ponder. In sixteen years he gained a wife and six children – and lost that wife and three of the children. Fearful experiences. Interestingly, all the problems we have here were his 100 years ago.

From Ian's diary May 1977:

The day after tomorrow is a big day, because it's the day the Senior Registrar's committee meet at St Mary's. I was interested to hear the other day that David Hamer has got a consultant job in Northampton. So that's really quite amazing, and it just makes one feel 'well, what if I'd stayed behind?' But there we are – that's all in the Lord's economy. I only wish, though, that I felt more that I was doing what the Lord wanted me to do at the present time. I think that tiredness, irritability, coupled with conflict, has made things more difficult for me. Last time I was very much prepared to regard myself as a sort of junior lad rushing about doing things. Now, of course, it's not that easy. I've been trained almost to consultant status, and I feel it much less easy to suffer the criticisms of people who aren't fully trained – it makes it more difficult. Still it's something one ought to bear in this work.

After Christmas 1976 Ian started to record his diary on tape in preference to writing it. A moving entry made in February 1977 reveals something of the extra cost of missionary service for those who have to part with their children for schooling at the age of six, or in some cases earlier. Rachel was five and three quarters when, on 2 February 1977, she left Bangkok for her first term at Chefoo School. Ian records the events of that time:

For days now we've been anticipating Rachel's departure with some apprehension. But she's still *been* here, so although we've felt the pain of it in a sense it's still been somewhat removed, like an operation that's coming but you've not yet felt any pain in the wound – it's just apprehension. She's been enjoying very much the 'farewells', the dinner under the house we had with the Parrys on Monday evening. Yesterday morning the day dawned and it was misty. We went down to Bangkok in the mist in the Toyota. I went down. I tried to get some shots of Rachel on the way with the telephoto lens. Once we arrived at Bangkok after a hot and sticky journey we went to Pan Road. There weren't all that number of people there actually, just a few children. We didn't spend long, just picking up a few things and unloading luggage, and I went off with Rachel to the British Club while Steph went with Mark to Central with the Townsends.

I remember as I walked up the road I was holding Rachel's hand. She was very hand-holdy that day – I'm not surprised. On the way up I asked her what she was thinking about, as she was rather quiet, and she said, 'You know,' and beyond that she wouldn't be drawn, so I didn't probe.

We got to the club and she changed and went in to bathe. It was really lovely. There were some more Chefoo people up there, and I think it was probably one of the best swims she's ever had. Repeatedly she climbed out and then jumped in with her wings. All I was able to do was a couple of lengths, but it was a most gorgeous sunny day. Then some others came, and we had a lovely lunch all together. After, there was more swimming, and Rachel was jumping off the spring-board and swimming to the side, and Mark was even doing it too – he had a wonderful time! I took some photos of them really enjoying themselves, and totally carefree. . . .

Then the time came – quarter to three. A bit sunburnt, we changed, and we walked, I think it's fair to say almost in silence, back to Pan Road, Rachel a little bit head down and trying to say things like, 'When we come back the first thing we'll do will be going to the British Club again.' Unequivocally now she was beginning to face the realities. We got to Pan Road and there were many more people there by now, and all the luggage was building up, and the Pickards arrived. Rachel was glad to see Naomi, but on this occasion Naomi herself was a little subdued, and they didn't have a great deal to say to each other. Nevertheless when something happened of an amusing nature, like Uncle Alex teasing some of them, she was prepared to join in the laughter.

Finally the bus, and all the luggage loaded, and the food parcels, and away we went to the station. So, platform tickets, and onto the big train. Rachel here was marvellously met by Carol Bevington, a little girl her own age, who took her by the hand and led her. They all got in, Steph helped Rachel find a place and they sat down. Rachel by this time had got her 'downy' (much loved remnant of her first eiderdown) and her blue bag. She was set up with Carol in a nice little slot, and of course they're very comfortable compartments. I took photographs, and we milled around for the best part of half an hour, until it was obviously just five minutes to go. Three minutes to go – Stephanie left, having said goodbye to Rachel. Then Rachel, off her own bat, came from her place, put her arm round Mark and gave him a kiss – it was very sweet – then walked up to me and gave me a big kiss, and we said 'goodbye'. No tears, just very serious about it.

Then we stood on the platform; several were in tears. In our window were the two Hillier boys and Carol and Rachel, all looking out of the same window. Suddenly, as we know it happens, the train moved off. Stephanie burst into sobs and I endeavoured to comfort her briefly. I shall never forget the look on Rachel's face as the train left – that funny, sort of half-guilty, shy look that she sometimes puts on. Sometimes when she's given a big present at Christmas she has that sort of look, because she's not sure what it is. It was that look of apprehension and yet half excitement, anticipation as she smiled as the train drew out – I hope I've captured it on film. Then I noticed Charles and John running along the platform holding the hands of their respective offspring, and so I decided to run along, and I caught the train up, and grabbed Rachel's hand, and ran along with her just for a few moments. And then 'good-bye, good-bye, *good-bye*' – for four and a half months.

I must confess that I had the greatest difficulty in restraining my emotions, and in the car that evening, there were times when tears seemed so easy to come. John was super. Having said good-bye to Anne, he took us to the airport and gave us a lovely meal. Mark was able to watch the airplanes, even though he was a bit tearful from being woken up, but that really was a little bit of a treat, and it just helped to mask our discomfort and anguish – anguish is the word, because, seeing that little girl with that little smile, totally unsuspecting of the reality of how long it was going to be. She probably thinks of it in terms of a month, or possibly a few weeks, but four and a half months – without her mummy or her daddy or her brother – it really is a terrible parting and separation. And John knew it. We were amazed to find when we got back, a card from Doff, a card from the Parrys, and then today a card from John with some milk (fresh milk a luxury) as a little gift. And people have been rallying round and saying how much they are with us in it. It's been quite remarkable to feel people helping us at this time.

The next evening:

Just about now, I'm speaking at eleven o'clock, the taxis will be arriving, or have arrived, at Chefoo. At the very minimum they'll be on the hill. Probably they've already got there, and they're having baths. I wonder how she's feeling now? This is the time – even now when she's tucked up in bed this evening, and she's arrived in a strange place, and we're miles away, maybe then she'll think, 'Oh I wish Mummy was here.' Well, Lord, we do commit her to you. We pray that you'll watch over her, and guard her in these days. It's an ache, as John said, rather like a bereavement. And yet we know only too well that, within possibly two or three weeks, we'll have adjusted, the letters will come through (we've written tonight). And then – the term will be on its way, things will be moving. At this particular time it's just parting; term hasn't really begun; she's still journeying away from us. But once the term is in progress, in a sense she's on her way back. At this moment she is on her way away, but from the moment we get our first letter, in a sense she's on her way back – and for that we'll praise the Lord!

After an initial homesickness Rachel settled well at Chefoo, coming home at the end of that first term with the ability to read to Mark, and a school report which said, 'Rachel has been a joy to teach.'

By June of 1977 Ian had mastered the Thai language sufficiently well to be able to give a talk to the Thai Christian nurses. He was, of course, nervous about this, and the evening before, when Mark was saying his prayers with Stephanie, she suggested that together they should ask Jesus to help Daddy with this Thai talk tomorrow. Mark's response: 'Does Jesus know Thai then?'!

In his last taped diary (no diary material found after June 1977), Ian says:

This week has been marked by intensive preparation for tomorrow morning's prayers. Mrs Prajat came round and we spent about two hours going through it, which was a great help. Then tomorrow she will be there to pray and read a passage before I speak. I think it will be just around ten minutes with the closing prayer. But what I am praying about is that, whatever the Thai is like, the teaching effect will be such that someone will be helped. I'm very conscious of the fact that at the present time my role out here has not yet been fulfilled. I've been a surgeon, doing perhaps more experienced surgery than others, but most of what I've done could have been done by others. Although it's been a relief to them, I've not, in a sense, really been fulfilling the task I've been called to. Certainly tomorrow morning will be a step on the way, and I really have asked the Lord to make my life more of a blessing to others, in a sense the starting point, a new beginning in my time here in Thailand. I feel at times, as I was saying to Steph, almost like a man in a dream – a sort of break with the past. The other day I realised I couldn't remember what the treatment sheets looked like at St Mary's – bad news really. I'm waiting to hear how the meeting last Tuesday afternoon, 31 May went, vis-à-vis my extension to stay in Thailand. And I pray, and I'm sure that the Lord will overrule and allow that. We've had some encouraging letters from home, and we're looking forward to my parents, and Steph's parents, coming out in about six months' time. Rachel is coming home next week! It's really exciting – I know Steph can't wait, and Mark certainly can't.

It really is quite amazing how *fast* this seventeen and a half weeks have gone. Unbelievable! I remember driving back after supper with John with tears in my eyes thinking, 'Well, she's gone for a long time.' And now *that really has gone*. 'Short as the watch that ends the night before the rising sun.' I just hope that my life, which I don't want to wish away, can be galvanised and remade into something worth while. With the passage of time so swift and so fleeting that seventeen weeks seem like one, one must surely take a grip of one's self and, with God's help, achieve something for him IN HIS TIME.

Though Ian, at the time of this diary entry, may have felt that his 'role had not yet been fulfilled', others were more aware of the contribution he had made to Manorom, as the following letter shows. It was written by John Townsend just as he was about to leave for furlough in September 1977:

Dear Ian and Steph,

Greetings from Field Council! It was good to have the opportunity, yesterday, to review your work and immensely valuable contribution here at Manorom during your time with us. We all want to express our appreciation, not only for the heavy load and responsibilities which you are carrying, but the way you have immersed yourself so fully in all that is going on, in terms of evangelism and direct contact with Thai friends and colleagues.

We appreciate your straightforward way, Ian, and natural gifts of leadership. We are going to miss you tremendously, but certainly realise the commitments you have back in England and wish you well in your career back home which I am sure will be a successful one. Back in England, whatever your situation both in consultant surgical practice and in church commitments, we feel that your experience out here will be something that you'll carry with you as something valuable, and as something that carries a whole set of fresh insights.

Countdown

One of the highlights for Ian and Stephanie in 1977 was the fact that all four parents were to be with them for Christmas. Stephanie's parents, John and Marjorie Baldock, flew out on 20 November, followed by Ian's parents a month later. The story of that three weeks immediately prior to the accident is told by Ian's mother, with the aim of showing how, in various incidents, in retrospect one can see the Lord's hand pointing forward to what was to happen.

* * *

December 1977. We were off to Thailand for three weeks! We hadn't intended to go, in spite of much pleading from Ian and Stephanie. Owing to the intense heat, Christmas would be the only suitable time for a visit. The first Christmas the family would only just have gone; the second they would be nearly coming home – or so we thought. But as the weeks went by and 1977 dawned, we began to feel a compulsion to go, a sense of rightness about it, and arrangements began to be made. Plans made

62

from home, and also at Manorom, all fell into place so easily that, one day, during that summer, I said to myself, 'Our visit to Thailand is all working out so easily; I wonder if anything is going to happen?' If anyone had asked me what I thought *could* happen, I would have answered, 'Well, maybe one of us isn't going to be around when they return.'

20 December. The weather was dismal and misty as we left Heathrow that morning, but as we soared above the clouds into the sunlight, our spirits rose – we were on our way! Our luggage consisted mainly of gifts for Christmas, many articles required for the new baby expected in February, two chocolate Father Christmases with which to greet the children, and three pounds of brussels sprouts, specially requested by Steph, and kept as cool as possible; this meant tucking them between the two layers of double glazing in the overheated hotel bedroom over-night! The flight, in a DC 10 of Thai International, was uneventful and pleasant, and after seventeen hours, Bangkok at last – exciting beyond words!

Ian was waiting for us with Mark, Steph staying behind with Rachel who was recovering from a tummy upset. The plane was late, and Ian had amused Mark by trying to run up a 'down' escalator, resulting in a cut toe! He had borrowed the OMF minibus, and drove us for some thirty minutes through the appalling traffic and heat of Bangkok. I remember the canal by the side of the road, with what looked like floating green balloons, afterwards discovered to be water melons; men fishing up to their knees in water, and women in their colourful pars (long skirts) and 'lampshade' hats sweeping the road, or resting on their brooms.

On arrival at the OMF Guest House at Pan Road we were greeted by Rachel and Stephanie and her parents. The house was a large, pleasant, two-storey building, built on three sides of a square with grassed area and trees in the centre, and with a swing and slide for the children. I was struck by the somewhat spartan nature of the house, having to remove my shoes before entering, the lack of carpets, netting instead of window glass, the bathroom of stone floor and walls, with a cold shower coming from the latter – in short, my first taste of life in the tropics. Our bedroom was one in a row opening off a long balcony, overlooking the garden. It was a comfortable room, containing all we needed, and on the chest of drawers was a basket of orchids and a Christmas card on which Ian had written:

> 'Cool' Season's Greetings and best wishes for a
>   happy new year –
> Christmas in Thailand 1977
> Thank you for coming!

In the dining room lunch was served. On a long wooden table various dishes of curry were laid, and the inevitable bowl of rice, all of which we ate with spoons. There were bottles of soft drinks in the fridge which we could buy as extras, and we could eat in the dining room or take our meal out to a table on a shady patio in the garden – all very free and easy. I soon realised that this house had everything that was needed for those who lived here, and the many missionaries constantly in transit – no particular luxuries, but, above all, a warm welcome for all who came and went, and the relaxed sense of being at home with the OMF family.

After a much-needed afternoon sleep we went by taxi (they were cheap and plentiful) to the English Anglican Church to watch a children's Christmas nativity pageant. The centre of the church had been cleared, leaving a rectangular arena in which the children performed, passing the microphone from one to the other as they spoke their parts. The high spot for our children was the inclusion of a real donkey on which 'Mary' was seated. Mark was particularly impressed, and was quick to tell people afterwards, 'D'you know what? They had a *real* donkey in the church.'

That night we were too tired to do other than sleep well, in spite of the appalling noise of the traffic outside, relieved at this time between midnight and 4 am owing to the curfew still operating, following the recent student uprising.

Thursday 22 December. This was the day that Ian had planned to show us something of the tourist sights of Bangkok, so after a morning browsing round some of the shops, we left the rest of the family behind at Pan Road, arranging to meet them at the tour bus station later. The 'cool' season had let us down and the weather was blisteringly hot. We went with Ian in a river bus to see the King's Palace, with its superb architecture and colours, much of it overlaid with gold, spectacular in the sunshine and a tourist's paradise. We visited the temple holding the great image of the reclining Buddha, dusty and unimpressive except for its size and the intricate designs on the soles of its feet. Then on to the temple of the emerald Buddha, where the small greenish figure was enthroned high up above a sort of altar. Photographs were forbidden here, but we could sit on the floor and rest provided that our toes were not pointing towards the Buddha, which would have been a cultural offence. We took a taxi through the cultural and business areas of Bangkok, past the University so recently the scene of bloodshed, and arrived at the bus station in a state of near exhaustion. Ian found seats for us, and fetched us ice-cold reviving drinks. On boarding the bus we met up with the rest of the family, and set out for our real destination – Manorom Hospital.

The tour bus was excellent, air conditioned and with

washing and toilet facilities. There was an attractive Thai girl who acted as a sort of 'conductor', serving us with iced drinks, cakes presented on little frilly paper doileys, and perfumed tissues to refresh us. The journey of 125 miles took about two and a half hours, and it seemed to us that we were travelling along one long straight road relieved only by the occasional petrol-filling station. On either side was a view of endless paddy fields, flat and uninteresting, with coconut palms on the horizon standing stark against the sky like sweeps' brushes, and, as the darkness descended rapidly, tiny points of light appeared in the little villages in the 'sticks' beyond the rice. It was so cool in the bus that it was hard to believe that outside the atmosphere would be oppressively hot.

At last, our destination. The bus came to a halt and out we clambered, the sudden heat enveloping us like a warm blanket. We had arrived in darkness but there was the familiar sign we had seen on many photographs – 'Manorom Christian Hospital'. A straight sandy road, about 200 yards long, led up to the hospital compound, and Ian had arranged with Peter Farrington, the young dental surgeon, to meet us at the bus-stop with the hospital minibus. We piled in with our luggage, Ian took over and drove us up through the compound to the far end, where we were to stay all together, in one of the wooden houses on stilts, normally occupied by Drs John and Anne Townsend, now on furlough.

In the darkness we could see very little of the hospital itself that night. Our main impression was of being deposited in the middle of a jungle, trees all round us, and the air filled with the noises of a tropical night, the chirrups and croaks of crickets and frogs rising above the rest. It wasn't until morning that we realised that we were only a few yards from a wooden paling fence which separated the hospital grounds from the rice fields.

The house itself was spacious and pleasant, made entirely of wood, and with large fans in the ceilings which were adjustable at the touch of a switch. We had, in usual Thai custom, to leave our shoes outside and climb a wooden staircase to the entrance, but half way up, at a lower level, was the little wooden kitchen separate from the house, presumably against fire risk. Thankfully we sat down to the meal which awaited us, prepared by Noi, the enigmatic, unsmiling, but efficient Thai house girl. Rachel was asked to say 'grace', which she did in good measure, thanking the Lord Jesus for bringing Granny and 'Pop' safely here, and praying that we might all have a happy Christmas together. I realised for the first time how this small girl had grown spiritually over the last year.

We soon adapted to the strangeness of beds without blankets or duvets, tucking ourselves in under mosquito nets (mozzy nets, according to the children), the noises of the night outside and, above our heads, the whirring of the fan and the chirrup of small lizards, geckos, which lived around the ceiling without bothering us. This house was luxury, by missionary standards, having a normal shower room with flush sanitation, though without running hot water. However, Ian had fixed up a system whereby a bucket with holes in the bottom, filled with warm water, was pulled up by a rope on a pulley – thereby one could have the semblance of a warm shower.

Friday 23 December. We rose much earlier than at home. There didn't seem anything to stay in bed for – the sun was shining and the family was up and about at 7 am. Our bedroom opened onto a wooden balcony which ran along one side of the house. Here, each morning, we were to deposit our washing, and after breakfast Noi could be seen squatting at the foot of the staircase in the shade of the house, rubbing away with two large bowls of water and suds, hanging the clothes on a line, and subsequently

ironing and having them ready to wear at 4 pm – one of
the blessings of the tropics!

After breakfast of cereals, sticky rice and strange fruits,
we were able to take a look at our surroundings, wander
down the path through the area of missionary houses
similar to our own, with their brightly coloured flower
beds tended by one of the Thai women employed by the
hospital, and on past others more modern in style and
known affectionately by their occupants as 'Carnaby
Street'. We were impressed by the modern hospital buildings, the nurses' home and training school, and even from
the little that we saw at this stage the obviously high
standard of procedure being carried out.

In the heat of the afternoon we rested in the shade
under the house, on wicker chairs in various stages of
dilapidation, the one other piece of furniture being a table
made from a large cable reel, on its side and painted red.
We watched the children as they splashed in and out of
the portable ten-foot-wide swimming pool, a gift which
had been sent to the Townsends, and coming over to be
rubbed down with a towel, carefully avoiding the stream
of large ants foraging in a seemingly endless crocodile –
they had been known to bite! The mosquitoes made themselves felt, and we became familiar with 'mozzy bites',
'mozzy pills', 'mozzy doors' and windows covered with
'mozzy nets'. As we sat there that afternoon, drinking tea
or cold drinks, a tiny elfin figure appeared round the
corner of the house, and was welcomed into the group.
This was two-and-a-half-years-old Adèle, the youngest
child of Bryan and 'Twink' Parry, who lived close by.
Stephanie was very fond of her as, in her mind, she helped
to take the place of her little niece Sarah whom she had
left behind in the UK.

That evening of the 23rd we were to join in a 'Thai
Feast', a special Christmas event, a meal followed by films

in the compound, for the benefit of all the hospital staff. Long tables laden with Thai 'goodies' were prepared – for nurse aides, doctors, missionaries and staff, over 200 in all, and dressed in their 'best'. We mingled with the crowd, and Ian and Stephanie fetched us each a plate divided into sections containing food, none of which we recognised, except for an orange, plus a drink which looked like pale pink water and tasted like weak ink! It didn't matter that we only ate the orange – one had only to put one's plate down and someone else would soon benefit by a 'second helping'. I was standing under a tree, and suddenly felt something fall into my hair and wriggle. Frantically I tried to remove it, without any success, but it soon extricated itself, fell to the ground and ran away – a large black beetle! By this time I'd had enough, and it was back to the house for cheese on toast, a simple dish but a luxury at Manorom. Cheese was diffi-cult to come by, generally being brought back from a visit to Bangkok, and very expensive. There was one occasion, though, when a special consignment arrived for the mis-sionaries. It had been sent by the Canadians to the Cambodian refugees, who had rejected it with the message 'this soap's no good'!

Christmas Eve, and our first visit to Manorom Market, in reality a long village street lined with little shops mostly constructed of wood, and open-fronted with goods displayed outside. We were surprised to see famil-iar groceries in one of the shops, even the '57 variety' kind, but very much more expensive. There were goods of wicker and wood, and many attractive brightly coloured materials. The butcher's shop consisted of numerous fatty joints, mostly pork, suspended from a wooden bar and covered with flies. We moved on! This village was about half a mile from the hospital, and trans-port was usually by *samelor*, a tricycle with a seat for two behind the rider. To be pedalled down the road and back in this fashion was a pleasant experience, a refreshing breeze fanning one's face. The journey each way always cost three baht (about 9p). 'Don't ever pay more because, if you do, you'll make it difficult for the missionaries,' we were told.

We spent the afternoon preparing for Christmas, putting up decorations, and being introduced to friends who dropped in to bring small gifts. In the next house along the compound path lived Dr Bryan Parry with his wife Iona (or Twink, as she was always called), and three children, Matthew (six), Rebecca (four) and Adèle (two), and another baby due in January. Bryan was a young New Zealand surgeon, a very valuable second to Ian and one to whom Ian was eager to give experience. Twink, dark haired and attractive, was outgoing with plenty of initiative. Steph wrote in one of her letters: 'Twink is always thinking of things to do, and we tend to tag along.' And this 'thinking of things to do' was a great help in a situation where these young wives were often lonely, with their husbands spending so many long hours in the operating theatre (or O Room as it was called).

The Parry family were off to Hua Hin for a fortnight's holiday, starting early Christmas morning, so had invited our two families, eight of us, for carols, Christmas cake and coffee round the tree on the evening before. We went over at about 6 pm. Bryan, with his curly red-gold hair and large smiling eyes, met us at the top of the steps and welcomed us into the house. The living room, similar to our own, was full of the atmosphere of Christmas, accentuated by the soft glow of the candles and the brilliance of the lights on the tree round which we gathered. Bryan played his flute and Twink a small harmonium. The children sat on the floor or on our laps, and as we sang old and well-known carols, my vivid memory is of a scene radiant with the spirit of Christmas and the love of the family. All too soon it was over. We went back to our house, and we didn't see the Parrys again until the day we left Manorom when I went to say 'good-bye' to Twink and to wish her well.

Christmas Day 1977; Stephanie's thirtieth birthday. 5 am, and from all around the hospital compound missionaries and their families, and members of the staff, gathered together at the top of the main staircase in the hospital. We were each presented with a lighted candle, pushed through a disc of cardboard to catch the drips, and with these we wended our way in a long crocodile, singing the Christmas story in Thai, for those who could, and la-la-la for the rest of us. For many of those patients it must have been the first time they had heard the wonderful story of the babe of Bethlehem. After touring the wards we paraded slowly round the compound, singing as we went. Then, some thirty minutes later, it was back to breakfast, then down to the river beyond the village for what was, to many, the most important event of the day – the baptism of five new believers.

One of the Christian hospital staff lived in a little wooden house on stilts about twenty yards out from the river bank, and the baptisms took place in his 'front garden'. Pastor Surapon from the Thai Church officiated and there were five candidates, four men and one girl. Each stood on the river bank and gave their testimony before baptism, and, as they rose from the water, stood for a few moments while the pastor prayed. There was a crowd standing around, many of the missionaries, also local market people watching curiously. One of the candidates was a man who had been admitted some months before with gunshot wounds of face and jaw, and Ian and Peter Farrington together had repaired the damage. He had been so impressed by the love of Christ as shown through the hospital staff, plus the message of the gospel, that he declared himself to be a believer, and had asked for baptism. This was particularly rewarding for Ian and Peter.

11 am. The service in the little Thai church commenced with a nativity play performed by the local children, and was enjoyed by a packed church with an overflow of spectators craning their necks through the open windows. The usual Sunday sermon followed, given this day by a visiting Chinese pastor, speaking in Thai. Ian was able to interpret quietly, and the text was Romans 12:1 – 'I beseech you therefore, brethren, by the mercies of God, that ye present your bodies a living sacrifice, holy, acceptable unto God, which is your reasonable service.' The following Sunday we were to be away in northern Thailand for the weekend, but heard later that another pastor had preached at Manorom, again on Romans 12:1 – 'I beseech you therefore, brethren, that ye present your bodies a living sacrifice . . . your reasonable service.' The third Sunday, our last, yet another pastor preached, and his text was Romans 12:1 – 'I beseech you, therefore, brethren, that ye present your bodies a living sacrifice . . . your reasonable service.' Ian remarked, 'I wonder why we've had the same text three Sundays running?' It was many months later that, reading through Ian's diaries, I came across his entry on his thirty-first birthday; 'as a consecrated man offering myself a living sacrifice – my reasonable service'.

Christmas dinner was just like Christmas dinner at home, only for 'turkey' read 'chicken'. It didn't seem unnatural for the weather to be hot, though a bit too hot with temperature in the nineties, the overhead fans keeping us fairly comfortable. The meal was followed by the usual excitement of present-opening round the tree, listening to a recording of the Queen's speech, playing with newly discovered toys and games, tea and Christmas cake, and eventually, when the children were asleep under their nets and darkness had fallen, other missionaries drifting over to the house for a time of fellowship – and we talked and drank coffee to the accompaniment of the usual nightly chorus of crickets, frogs and geckos. Among those who were there were Gwenda Mills, a senior nursing sister from New Zealand, and Dr Julia Brown, a young paediatrician, both of whom were so soon to figure prominently in our lives.

Ian loved background music, whether in the home or when operating. A vivid memory of that Christmas Day is of two tapes that were played repeatedly. One was a medley of Christmas carols and songs, and the other, and more importantly, was a tape recording of the Chefoo children singing. One of their songs could never be forgotten. We imagined we could hear Rachel's strong little voice among the rest, as they sang:

> Come and go with me to my Father's house,
> To my Father's house, to my Father's house,
> Come and go with me to my Father's house
> Where there's JOY, JOY, JOY.
>
> It's not very far to my Father's house,
> To my Father's house, to my Father's house,
> It's not very far to my Father's house
> Where there's JOY, JOY, JOY.
>
> Jesus is the light in my Father's house,
> In my Father's house, in my Father's house,
> Jesus is the light in my Father's house
> Where there's JOY, JOY, JOY.

This truth of Jesus being the light must have made a big impression on Rachel. Three weeks later, as we sat in the air-conditioned foyer of a large hotel in Bangkok, sheltering from the blistering heat while waiting for a bus, a vast chandelier with hundreds of lamps suddenly sprang into light. 'D'you know?' said Stephanie, turning to me with a smile, 'Granny, that's the biggest light in the world!' 'Oh no!' said Rachel solemnly. 'Mummy, *Jesus* is the biggest light!'

Monday 26 December, Boxing Day for us, but a normal working day for the Thai, was spent quietly: helping Rachel to make a bead necklace, writing letters, sitting under the house. Having now been at Manorom for a few days, we were noticing how trying Mark had become, fractious and difficult to please. I noted this in my diary.

Tuesday 27, and I recorded: 'Beautiful day again – loving it here.' This was Ian and Stephanie's eighth wedding anniversary. They chatted about the future, their return to the UK in the coming September, and of Ian's need for a car – and what sort he would be able to afford. He also spoke with some frustration about the fact that his work on deep vein thrombosis had still not been published, and he planned to talk this over with his 'Chief' a few months later when they were due to meet at a medical conference in Singapore.

We wandered through the hospital compound, watched by curious eyes as people waited patiently in OPD (out-patients' department), or sat on the stone steps outside with their children playing around them, and returning our smiles as we passed. Mid-morning we went over to the Farringtons' house for coffee. Peter was English, and his wife Rosemary Australian, and they lived in a house on the main road outside the compound with their two boys, Johnny (five) and Ben (two and a half). Rosemary's parents, Jock and Joan Kennedy, had also come out to be with their family for Christmas. It was a happy hour, though Rosemary was suffering with back strain and was in a certain amount of pain. We chatted while the children played together, and Ben took advantage of adult conversation to return to the goodies on the table! Johnny was soon to go to Chefoo School. I had met him briefly a few days earlier, and when I was introduced to him I was arrested, almost startled, by the look in his big wide eyes. I remember thinking as I looked at him, 'you have heaven in your eyes; you look as if you're half there already', a flash of thought vividly brought to mind later, when I learned that Johnny had, in fact, become interested in heaven. The night before the accident he was asking his mother what heaven would be like, and she had shown him her diamond ring in an effort to explain how beautiful it would be. Johnny wasn't the only one showing this interest, either. One lunch-time during that week Ian started a conversation about heaven. He said that someone had stated that we shouldn't expect rewards in heaven, but that it was his opinion that we should, because the Scriptures told us it was so. Ian believed the promises, and said, 'I certainly am looking forward to that.'

Through this fortnight, as Bryan was away, Ian was only off duty when away from the hospital. So the internal telephone (there was no contact with the outside world) was constantly ringing and Ian would speak, sometimes in English, sometimes in Thai, according to the caller. This often meant a hasty return to the hospital, but never too often for Ian. I can remember one particular occasion, late at night, when he received a message about a patient so ill that he should have been seen much sooner, and he sat back and laughed, with a mixture of disbelief and exasperation saying, 'Why, oh why don't they send for me sooner? They know I don't mind being called at any hour of the day or night.' (Ian had, in fact, a reputation for 'being as bright at 2 am'.)

Wednesday 28 December. We all, the family plus Stephanie's parents and ourselves, went by taxi, a very suspect vehicle, to Nakhon Sawan, a large and busy town about sixty kilometres from Manorom, to visit Grace Harris, an OMF missionary working mainly among children. Her shady and pleasant little house was set well back from the road, with a garden rich in tropical trees and beautiful hibiscus flowers. Grace welcomed us warmly to a meal of various Thai dishes attractively served, and we were introduced to new delicacies not all to our liking, e.g. bean curd which, to our palates, resembled small squares of lard, relished, however, by the others. As we sat around and chatted, the voices of many children floated through the door and windows, the primary school being next door. We were shown round the little house, up a wooden staircase to Grace's pleasant bedroom, and experienced a measure of culture shock when introduced to her washing and toilet facilities, primitive and far removed from the more updated arrangements at Manorom! Soon it was time to return. The taxi arrived to pick us up, but the journey back was interrupted by the car running out of petrol owing to a leaking tube. The driver borrowed a motor bike from a passing traveller, and we sat by the roadside in the sweltering heat for twenty minutes, sheltering against the shady side of the taxi from the blazing sun.

Thursday 29 December. The temperature was still in the nineties, so we were not sorry to be off to Chiang Mai in northern Thailand to spend the New Year weekend at 'Pinecrest'. In the morning the children had a great time in the pool, Rachel's swimming improving every day. At 8 pm a taxi called for us, and it was at this point that we had to say 'goodbye' to Stephanie's parents who were returning to the UK. We would miss them – we had all been so happy together, and as we sped off in the taxi Rachel cried a lot. Mark added, 'I'm missing Mussle' (the cat!). The taxi, again a very suspect vehicle, took us along the Asian Highway to the railway station at Paknam Pho, where we were to catch the night train to Chiang Mai. We arrived on time, as we thought, only to find that Ian had mistaken the time of the train, and we had an hour to wait. The air was hot and oppressive, the station gradually filling with people, on the platform stalls offering various Thai delicacies, drinks and sticky sweetmeats. Dogs were lying around asleep, for which I was thankful. I always suspected that Thai dogs were stray or rabid or both, mainly, I suppose, because they looked skinny and didn't have collars. We sat on our cases and the only available wooden seat, and little Thai children crept curiously up to our children's little white faces, wanting to touch them, fascinated by these unusual strangers. At last the train arrived and we clambered aboard to find our reserved seats and, as earlier on the tour bus, were agreeably surprised. The standards of cleanliness and comfort were excellent, and I slept as never before on a night train. We arrived at Chiang Mai in the morning to a much cooler atmosphere after a heavy overnight rainfall. The OMF minibus was there to meet us, and we drove to the Guest House for breakfast.

The morning was spent exploring the special attractions of the town, the woodwork shop where beautiful articles could be bought very cheaply, the workshops behind where we watched the girls chipping away at the intricate carving, the silver and jade shop next door where I was invited to choose a brooch for my 1978 birthday, followed by an hour spent in the vast, two-storey, covered-in market where one could find an abundant choice of gifts to take back to the UK.

Ian, having borrowed the OMF minibus for two days, drove us up a winding road through wooded country for about 2,000 feet, until, on turning a corner, we came upon 'Pinecrest', this lovely OMF retreat, remote and cool, with a balcony at the back where one could sit for meals and look down to the woods sloping away behind the house, and out over Chiang Mai to the misty hills beyond. This weekend our family had again linked up with David and Sue Pickard and their children. The Pickards had arrived the day before, and had prepared well for us, with English food, and generously allocating us the best room. We slept well that night, my only concern being an army of ants which paraded endlessly along a ledge on the wall behind our bed, so we moved the bed out a foot or so to avoid a night invasion!

Saturday 31 December. The day dawned pleasantly cool and sunny, and we had breakfast on the balcony before setting out to visit one of the Blue Meo tribal villages. Ian drove us in the minibus another 1,000 feet up a very bumpy road, to a plateau from which we had to descend about a mile down a muddy track to the village. Overnight rain had made the ground unsafe to venture any further, but, at this moment, to our relief, a *songtaow* (open-backed truck with seats on either side) arrived with several Thai on board, also going to the village, which was sufficiently near civilisation to be a tourist attraction. The driver agreed to allow us to join their party for 100 baht (about £3), and down we went.

The villagers were obviously fairly used to tourists. Several of them were dressed in their traditional finery, brightly coloured and braided blouses and long skirts, children with hats that looked like the product of Christmas crackers, only made of cotton and beautifully ornamented; a little girl with her brother on her back and her wealth around her neck – numerous silver necklets reputed to be made from coins brought across the border from Burma. There were many stalls with innumerable trinkets to be bargained for, and the inevitable cane and woodwork, all against a background of leaf-roofed huts, a communal water tap, and pigs and dogs wandering in unfettered freedom. We thought, 'How difficult it must be to attempt to evangelise these people,' and yet we knew it was happening and people were finding Christ, even in places such as this.

The time came for the *songtaow* to ascend the hill. The driver attached chains to the wheels, but half way up the hill they fell off. We were all asked to get out, which we did, whereupon a small Meo boy leapt off the roof, on which he had installed himself down in the village, evidently anticipating just this incident and ready to help, thereby earning himself a few baht.

Presently we arrived at the spot where we had left our vehicle, and Ian drove us up several hundred feet higher, coming out onto a clearing dotted with tree stumps, and commanding a wonderful view down over the little 'doll-sized' village from which we had come, and, in the other direction, the beginning of the Himalayan range stretching away to the horizon. The air was warm with a soft breeze. We made a fire and cooked sausages, which we ate with salad and fruit, cake and coffee. Then, as Ian wanted us to have the maximum of impressions, a drive still higher, and a woodland walk to get a view of the King's Summer Palace, its roof glistening gold in the sunshine.

The drive down was terribly bumpy, and I was really concerned for Steph whose baby was due in February. But all was well – it had been a lovely outing. In the evening the children, organised by Rachel as usual, acted their version of 'Goldilocks and the three bears', followed by a good English meal of roast meat, and games round the fire.

While we had been enjoying the freedom and holiday atmosphere of this lovely day, we didn't know until later that a seventeen-year-old Thai Christian boy, once a leprosy patient, returning from a day of prayer for the special evangelistic campaigns planned for 1978, had been involved in a traffic accident, thrown out of the vehicle in which he lay on the floor sleeping, and killed instantly – an incident which was to become to us unforgettable.

Sunday 1 January 1978. After a rather chilly night we awoke to another lovely morning, and to a hubbub of noise from the road some 200 yards below, as folk came up the hill in coachloads to celebrate the New Year by climbing the hundreds of steps to the beautiful temple of Door si Tep, there to 'make merit' as they burned their joss sticks and bowed to the figure of Buddha.

In the morning David Pickard gathered the children together in a little Sunday school class among the trees, below the balcony at the back of the house, and we watched as little hands were raised eagerly in answer to his questions. In the evening, when the children were in bed, we adults had fellowship and prayer around the fireside, and Ian read to us from Jim Packer's book *Knowing God*. I remember him saying, 'Every paragraph in this book is a good value.' He also read from *Every Day with George Duncan*. I remember his reading a passage that night which stated that 'when deep trouble comes it is not wrong for a Christian to ask why? – because on the cross the Lord Jesus cried, "My God, my God, why?"'

A month later, in the Thanksgiving service for the lives and work of Ian and Stephanie, at Leigh-on-Sea, the Rev. Nick Carr stood in the pulpit, and his first words were, 'My God, my God, why?'

Monday 2 January. This was the day we had to say 'goodbye' to 'Pinecrest'. After breakfast Ian went out to the balcony and stood alone and silent as he gazed out over the hills, thinking, no doubt, that it would be very unlikely that he would ever again be able to visit this, his favourite spot in Thailand. It was a long and tiring day as we travelled south by coach, the fare being cheaper than by train. There was no air-conditioning, we were uncomfortably hot, and there was no escaping the plaintive Thai music which wailed incessantly through the speaker in the roof. The driver drove fast, and perilously near the centre of the road. This gave me even more cause for concern when we stopped for lunch. We were parked in a large coach park littered with badly mutilated vehicles, and I tried not to think of what might have happened to the occupants! We walked across the road to an open restaurant where we sat at long wooden tables and were provided with a meal, all included in the bus fare, and second helpings if desired – I didn't eat my first! It was with considerable relief that our weary feet eventually climbed the steps to our house at Manorom. Ian went off to a meal, in response to an invitation from the hospital sewing lady. He was given a delicious Thai meal of many dishes, and there was good conversation in which he was able to take part. We too had been invited, but we declined politely. We were very tired, the food didn't appeal, and the conversation would have been pointless!

January 3, 4 and 5. During this first week in January we had opportunities to explore the hospital further, and to meet more of the missionaries who were offering us hospitality.

We sat in one of Ian's clinics, listened to a 'preach' in OPD, toured the wards, especially the maternity block where Stephanie wanted to see just where her baby would be delivered and to ask questions of Bernice White who was in charge. We were also able to watch Ian operating and that to music! Ian had decided that light music would have a relaxing effect on the tension of theatre work, and so had instituted taped music as an accompaniment to thyroidectomies, hernia and fracture repairs, etc.,

etc. This was greatly appreciated by the staff involved, and the custom continues, though at first causing slightly raised eyebrows among the senior missionaries!

It was during this first week in January that we began to notice a remarkable change in Mark. Instead of being a fractious, difficult little boy he became sweet and amiable, easy to play with and amenable to others. I thought, 'Mark, I have misjudged you. You are not the tiresome child of my first impressions; in fact you are a very lovable little boy.'

In another house along the compound path lived Lukas Juzi, youngest of the three sons of Ulrich Juzi, eye surgeon and Hospital Administrator, and his wife Adèle, Swiss-German missionaries. Ulrich takes up the story: 'In the weeks before the accident, Lukas asked repeatedly concerning life after death. These questions were surprising on two accounts: unusual for a five-and-a-half-year-old boy, and with no other reasons or events leading to such questions. Lukas has always been an easy, happy and humorous little boy. But in the last three weeks before the accident his obedience and behaviour reached an unusual degree, so that Adèle sometimes asked him, "Lukas, why are you so good?" She asked the Lord in her heart, "What is the meaning of this that Lukas is so good?" She remembered another boy who became very, very good shortly before he died and she felt disturbed in her heart.'

Away in Hua Hin, where the Parrys were on holiday, Twink was remarking to Bryan, 'D'you know, I can never remember a time when our family has been more united.' That must surely have denoted good behaviour on the part of the Parry children. So, quietly, God was preparing the little ones he was going to take to himself.

Thursday 5 January. On this evening, after a meal with three of the missionary nursing sisters in 'Carnaby Street', we went to a prayer and Bible study session in the nurses' auditorium. The visiting speaker that night was Mr Jim Tootill who, many years before, and unknown to us, had lost a little girl in a drowning accident at Manorom. He had felt impelled, as he later explained, to take as his text the words of Job: 'The Lord gave, and the Lord has taken away; blessed be the name of the Lord.' He spoke for an hour and I began to get restless, thinking of the others back at the house. But I looked round at the missionary staff who were there, drinking in every word, and I realised how valuable was this spiritual food in a life where good Christian teaching had to be obtained mainly from tapes. I didn't realise then that this particular message was for us and for those others who were to be bereaved, for, as I look back on that night, I remember that those who were to lose their loved ones, and who were at Manorom at the time, were all present, but all those who were to be taken were, for one reason and another, not able to be there.

Twelve years earlier, when studying Job, Ian had written in his diary: 'He uses the seeming disaster and tragedy to bring about his purposes. "Except a corn of wheat die. . . ." May I be prepared to face adversity.' He couldn't have known that he was writing it for us. The rest of that week was made up of 'the days of small things', sitting under the house talking, watching the children swimming, visiting the local market, while Ian worked on in the hospital, and in the evening we retired to the one air-conditioned bedroom for a game of 'Rook', to listen to music, or to see slides of Malaysia, just enjoying the family and valuing every precious minute as the days drew near to our departure. During the course of that week Ian, in conversation one day, said, 'I am out here for one reason only – that this is where God has told me to be.'

Saturday 7 January. Ian wanted to take us up river at Manorom village to visit a temple, from which there was a beautiful view over the river. We made our way to the quayside, where we would secure a noisy little motor boat and a man to drive it. An old lady, her face creased and scorched by the sun, was collecting the fares, and the usual bargaining began. A price was asked. 'Too much,' said Ian, 'I'm a poor man.' 'What?' said the lady, 'you come to this country and you speak our language? You must be rich.' Ian explained that for a missionary this was not the case. A price was agreed and off we sped, up the river, past little wooden dwellings on stilts at the river's edge, children diving in and out of the water, here and there a Buddhist temple glittering in the sun, the river widening as we went, and vegetation becoming sparse. There was breeze in our faces, refreshing and invigorating, spray which cooled us as the boat raced on, well compensating for the noise of the motor which made conversation impossible. We reached our destination and climbed a long flight of steps up a hill to where a statue of the Buddha sat with a silver 'umbrella' over his head, and the temple further up the hill behind him. We didn't stay long, just long enough to take photographs of the view, and of ourselves framed by an ornate stone archway over which tumbled an abundance of bougainvilia.

In the evening we walked through the compound to the farthest point from our house, to a spot known as 'Kiwi Corner', where two New Zealand missionary nursing sisters lived. One of these was Gwenda Mills, who was alone that night, and had invited us to a meal. We sat round a table on her wooden balcony, enjoying a delicious western-style salad meal with slices of fresh pineapple, and watched the sun go quickly down over the rice fields which stretched away to the main road with cars like fleeting glimpses of 'Dinky' toys in the distance.

Afterwards, the children having been taken back to bed, my husband and I stayed behind to talk with Gwenda, sitting in her small living room and watching fascinated as various insects swarmed round the lamp and many many more tried to get in through the netted window. Later, as we walked through the darkened compound, we were stopped and challenged by a guard whose presence was really more of a deterrent to casual thieves than a safeguard against bandits. We didn't know how to answer him, so he fell in behind us and followed us back to the house, whether to protect us or protect others from us we didn't quite know, but were very glad to reach the shelter of home and close the door firmly behind us!

Sunday 8 January. Our last day all together at Manorom. In the morning a few of the other missionaries came over to our house for a time of prayer and fellowship – about a dozen of us altogether. One of these was Noel Sampson, a young Australian surgeon, who, with his wife Louise had just come up from Bangkok for the birth of their second child, due in about ten days. At present they were engaged in language study, preparatory to Noel's taking Ian's place at Manorom in a few months' time. Before coming to Thailand, and after medical training, Noel and Louise had felt that Bible training was essential to their future missionary service, and had been for a course at All Nations Christian College. This completed they were now in Thailand with their small son Ben, planning to make missionary service their life work. Louise wasn't finding it easy, adjusting to the culture, the heat and the language. I don't think I spoke to her personally, but heard from others of her courage and serenity. During his time at All Nations, Noel had the opportunity to give his testimony at a Christmas service. This was taped, and it expresses the reality of his faith:

When I started my university course in medicine I was happy and thought all was well. You see, I didn't believe there was a God, because I didn't want there to be a God. I knew if there was a God he had a right to a 'say' in my life. I knew if there was a God then I needed to follow him, and I just wanted to live my life for myself. I thought, there's only one way to get the best out of life – and that's to do what I want to do. And so I had refused to believe that there was a God.

But, at Christmas time ten years ago, my girlfriend was going to a Christian camp, and the thought of it being a Christian camp didn't please me terribly much. I didn't particularly like the idea of prayer and Bible study, but the camp was being held on the Gold Coast in Australia, and that's a little like the French Riviera here; it's the place that everyone loves to go to for sun and sand and surf. And so I thought, 'That's such a good holiday I'll go, and I just won't listen to too much of what's being said.' When I went, the speaker there talked about sin, and I sat in the meetings and thought to myself, as he went through all these things, 'That's not me; other people have done things like that, but not me.' He said things like, 'You haven't got a meaning in life,' and I said, 'But of course I've got a meaning in life – I'm doing medicine. Surely that's one of the best meanings in life that I could have.' But as I got away on my own, and I really started to look honestly into my life, and I really started to think of what those nineteen years of my life had held, I began to realise that I hadn't even been living up to my own standards, let alone those standards which I knew were perfect standards. I realised that at the centre of my life there was just conceit and selfishness and self-centredness. As I sat there and listened to the presentation of Christianity, I began to realise that Jesus *was* alive, and that he was calling upon me to make a commitment to him.

Now I didn't have all my intellectual questions answered. I can't quite explain how it was, but I just knew that Christ was calling upon me to surrender my life to him, and to follow him, and to take him as the new boss of my life. Now you can imagine what that meant for me, having lived nineteen years of my life just for myself. I realised that to make a decision like that is a once and for all thing. I couldn't bear to make a decision like that and then three months later turn back on it. Then I wondered if I could live up to what I knew was the Christian standard of life. Then, one night, and I look back on the night with tremendous thankfulness, God enabled me just to ask Jesus to become my Saviour. To my amazement, I suddenly found that I had a relationship with Christ that was real and meaningful. I had always thought that being a Christian was following a set of rules, a set of do's and don'ts, a sort of dry, uninteresting life. But to my amazement there was a reality in knowing Christ, and there was a sense of joy and rightness with God that I never believed existed, and it came upon me with such a surprise. I can remember the moment that I realised it – I literally jumped for joy. It was fantastic! I want to say that God has enabled me to keep following him despite the fact that I didn't feel I ever could, and despite the fact that deep down inside I'm still the old 'me'. But I've found Christ real, and he's changed my life. There are many people who ask today, 'Is Christianity real? Is Christ who he claimed to be? Did he really rise from the dead? Can he really change lives today?' I tell you with all my heart, not because I read it in a book but because I know it in experience, yes – it's true! Jesus said, 'I am come that you might have life.' Isn't that strange to those who think that being a Christian loses all its joy? And more than that – God says in his word that 'he who has the Son has life, and he who has not the Son has not life'. I want to close by asking you a question. Do *you* have the Son living within you, and therefore do *you* have life, or somehow does this experience not seem real to you? Jesus says, 'I am come that *you* might have life,' and he wants you to respond to him and take him as the new master of your life.

So Noel was one of those present at the small house meeting on the morning of Sunday 8 January. Rosemary Farrington was there too, and Gwenda Mills, Ian and

Stephanie and the children, besides ourselves and two medical students doing their 'electives' at Manorom.

We had a time of prayer together, and Rosemary prayed especially for her two little boys. Ian prayed, 'Lord, strengthen me that while I stand firm on the rock and strong in thee, I may stretch out a loving hand to wrestlers with the troubled sea.'

One of the students prayed that he might find much work to do at Manorom, which brought forth an immediate response from Ian, 'Your prayer is answered already!'

Ian's father gave a short talk on Hezekiah and the incentive to serve, finishing with the well-known couplet,

> 'Only one life – t'will soon be past –
> Only what's done for Jesus will last.'

And for five of that small group, within one week life on earth *would* be past.

On the Sunday afternoon of the 8th the funeral service took place in the leprosarium chapel of the young Thai Christian who had been killed on the road a week earlier. It was an inspiration to see some patients crippled by leprosy, turning the pages of hymn books without fingers or even without a hand, but with the joy of the Lord in their faces. The father of the young man was there, and though not himself a believer, he spoke of the reality of his son's new-found faith and the difference it had made to his life. Following the service, the cremation had to take place at the Buddhist temple, down the road towards Manorom village. It was the only crematorium available, even for Christians, in the area. We and several of the missionaries went down to support the Christians at the committal ceremony.

The crematorium, at the side of the temple, was ugly and macabre. A few steps led up to a wooden platform surrounded by a railing, and, at the side opposite the steps, a dirty smoke-stained oven would be opened to receive the coffin. We and the young man's father, the pastor and other friends and relatives, gathered round the trestle on which the coffin had been placed, watched curiously from below by bystanders and Buddhist monks. The pastor, himself once a leprosy patient, gave a short and moving testimony to the fact that though this body might be burned, buried or thrown in the river, nothing could alter the fact that his spirit was alive and with the Lord, and spoke of the joy of the Christian hope. When it came to the actual disposal of the coffin, an official, who looked somewhat like the 'Mikado', started with hammer and chisel to open the coffin, much to our consternation. It was apparently the custom to burn the body and reuse the coffin when possible. However, on this occasion the procedure proved inadvisable, for which we were thankful!

That Sunday evening was our last all together at Manorom. The following morning Stephanie would have to take the children down to Bangkok for immigration registration, a constant and costly procedure for missionaries, and we were to follow with Ian on Tuesday. But this Sunday evening was our own, and we spent it in the air-conditioned room – a quiet, family evening – Mark asleep in the adjoining children's bedroom, Steph lying on the bed resting, one arm round Rachel as she read to her, and they talked about the new baby so soon to arrive. Ian wrote letters for us to take home, we talked, and drank coffee, and finished the evening with prayer and Ian's reading from *Day by Day with George Duncan*.

Monday 9 January. This was an uneventful day following Steph's departure on the tour bus to Bangkok, but it finished with one of Ian's busiest nights. After his evening ward round and a time with us, he said, 'I have to go back at 10 pm to do a Caesar.' We went to bed, alone except for the creatures that provided a perpetual concert in the night. It wasn't until the morning, when Ian appeared at breakfast as usual at 7 am, that we heard that he had been up until 5 am dealing with a road traffic accident. 'The worst I have ever had to cope with,' he said – severe multiple injuries from which the man subsequently recovered.

Ian then had a full day's operating, and at 4.30 we caught the tour bus to Bangkok, and linked up with Stephanie and the children.

Wednesday 11 January was set aside for what Ian described as 'pure tourism'. We visited the snake farm, and watched men handling these deadly creatures with ease, extracting from them venom to be used to make serum for snake-bite victims. In the afternoon we went out to the Rose Garden, where, in a vast auditorium, one could watch a wide variety of Thai culture: boxing, dancing, cockfighting (one round only!), Buddhist marriage ceremony and Buddhist monk initiation ceremony, and other demonstrations, since forgotten.

In the evening, while Rachel and Mark stayed with David and Sue Pickard, we took Ian and Stephanie to dinner at the revolving restaurant at the top of the Narai Hotel, with the magnificent panorama of Bangkok by night spread out before us. After the meal, over which we lingered to enjoy this last evening, Ian and Stephanie went back to the Pickards' house to collect the children. We stayed for a while to explore the beautiful little shops inside the hotel, and bought some last-minute gifts before strolling back to Pan Road. The family hadn't arrived back, so we prepared to go to bed in our room opening off the long balcony, the family room being the largest one at the far end. I was restless until they arrived and couldn't settle. At last I heard the sound of padding feet. I went out onto the balcony. Mark had run to his bedroom door and was curled up outside. I bent down and kissed him. Rachel was making her way sleepily down the balcony. For one brief moment, and for the last time, I held her close.

While Ian was in Bangkok, Bryan, now returned from Hua Hin, was carrying on the general surgery at Manorom. One night, a few days before the accident, he had a strange dream. He was gazing up into a vast mansion bathed in light, with a wide staircase winding up through the centre, and on this staircase was Twink, with the two little girls. In his dream Bryan thought,'Why am I not on the staircase, why not Matthew?' He remembered the dream vividly when he woke, and told Twink about it. They laughed together and it was forgotten – temporarily.

Thursday 12 January. We were up at 7 am for a trip up the river to see the Floating Market. We made our way down to Silom Street, over dangerously uneven paving stones and past obnoxious piles of rotting garbage. In Silom Street we were greeted by the usual early morning sight of monks with their begging bowls, collecting their day's supply of food from those who wished to 'make merit' by this offering.

We went up river for about thirty minutes in a large motor boat filled with tourists, and with an English-speaking guide. As the vegetation grew more lush, so the riverside homes looked less shabby. The people here were not very poor: they grew their own fruit and vegetables, and, in the early morning, launched out into the river with their boats laden with produce. In their Thai dress and hats they made a colourful sight. For the equivalent of a few pence our guide bought a large hand of bananas and threw them into the boat for us to divide among ourselves. The terminus, or turn-round point, was a large and very expensive indoor market or store where beautiful articles could be bought, but at a much inflated price. 'Don't buy anything,' we were told – an unnecessary piece of advice, for by this time we were practically out of baht! On the way back, small boys, nimble as fishes, swam up to the boat and begged for coins. Swiftly leaving them behind, we stopped for a while to disembark to see Wat Arun, the Temple of the Dawn, made up of tiny innumerable mosaics and reputed to be one of the most beautiful buildings in the world. One could ascend nearly to the top by a steep external flight of steps. Ian and the children went up about half way – we waited below in the heat.

Immediately after lunch, while the rest of us had a siesta, Ian finished writing a short commentary for a set of slides which he was sending home with us, to be shown at a Christian Medical Fellowship meeting in London. With his final slide he wrote:

> I end with the dawn not sunset, because 1978 may in a very real sense be the dawn spiritually for thousands, and we need much prayer. There has been much sowing, but little general reaping. It is a year of major campaigns and outreach for the Thai Church. Could it be that in this year, like the dawn over the rice fields at Manorom, we shall see the light of the sun of righteousness spread over this eastern land as yet in spiritual darkness? Pray that it may be so.

That final task accomplished, we all went to the British Club for the family to have a last swim before catching the tour bus back to Manorom. I remember the children throwing themselves into the clear blue water with complete abandon, followed, for them, by a meal of egg sandwiches and chips (real English type, not sweet potatoes), and they argued over who should have the last few chips. Ian swam, while we sat and talked with Steph. All too soon it was time to go. Steph held Mark's hand and I held Rachel's as we threaded our way through the traffic and the people, for the family to catch the local bus to the tour bus station. But, too late, it had just gone. So, quickly, Ian hailed a taxi, we hurriedly kissed, and they were off, waving 'good-bye' and 'see you in September'. I remember noticing particularly Mark's shy, trusting little smile for us as he climbed into the car. Slowly we made our way back to Pan Road, a little sad, but not too much so. After all, September was only eight months away, and there would be letters every week.

* * *

We arrived at Heathrow on Friday morning, full of our wonderful time in Thailand – and it *had* been a wonderful time. I had thought as we travelled to the airport at Bangkok, 'What a happy three weeks it has been – nothing to mar it.' In a letter to a friend written during that week, Ian had said, 'It has all gone so well but so quickly, and sadly they leave on Thursday.'

Suffering from 'jet lag' it wasn't difficult for us to get to sleep on Friday night. At 4 am (11 am Bangkok time) I awoke with a feeling of intense oppression bearing down upon me. I said to myself, 'Why am I feeling like this? Must be reaction from the flight.' I committed it to the Lord, praying to be released from it. I was – and soon fell asleep again.

On Saturday evening the telephone rang – and we heard.

Letters every week? Yes, they had come every week during Ian's total of two and a half years in Thailand, none more than a few days late. Now there were to be no more – except *one*. By the first post after the accident there arrived a letter from Ian, marked AIR MAIL in large letters and correctly stamped. It had been posted on 31 October 1977 and had taken two and a half months to arrive. In it Ian was describing what happens when there is a road accident in Thailand. He said, 'Out here it's always the person in the bigger vehicle who is responsible – always!' Coincidence? Unbelievable? Rather that the Lord had held this particular letter up in order to set his seal on what the OMF had already told us – that there was no way in which Ian, who was driving, could possibly have prevented the accident.

Saturday 14 January was Children's Day in Thailand, and so a special outing was arranged. The Lord saw to it that there was one adult, and only one, Rosemary Farrington, who remembers clearly, and she takes up the story:

I'll tell you the events of the morning beforehand. Steph had arranged with me to go up, and I was going to have lunch with them because Peter was going to Nakon Sawan to do visitation for The Thrust (the 1978 campaigns), and so we were going to spend the day together. Ian rang that morning and said, 'We're going to Phao-Ha. Do you want to come too?' I said, 'Yes, we would like to come.' So we'd gone up, and then we met over at Twink's place for a cup of coffee. Different people had heard about the trip and everybody wanted to go. Twink said, 'Can we go?' Then the Sampsons heard about it and wanted to go, because the rice barges being loaded at harvest is quite a sight and good for photos. Then Julia heard about it and wanted to come, and apparently my Johnny invited Jonathan and Lukas Juzi to come, and eventually Adèle said they could. We were beginning to be quite a vanful, but we weren't overloaded, and so we set off. We had a lovely morning: stopped on the way and took some photos of threshing floors and winnowing, and then we got there. The children were enjoying themselves because there were great heaps of rice. The people were carrying it on to the barges, in baskets on sticks carried over their shoulders, and the children were helping by scooping it up in handfuls to fill the baskets. They were really hindering rather than helping, but they looked so cute, and the people were so taken with them, and my memory is of just taking a picture of Johnny, just catching him in my viewfinder, scooping up the rice and hopping about, and I remember seeing the group of children standing on the river bank, watching the barges. They were beautiful children, they really were! It's hard to imagine that, just in a moment, so many of them went, but it's wonderful to have confidence in where they are. Rachel and Mark Gordon-Smith, Becky and Adèle Parry, Johnny Farrington, Lukas Juzi, Ben Sampson and three unborn babies.

About the actual accident. The facts are that we were coming along the road towards Manorom. Ian was driving perfectly safely, not fast. Noel had just said, 'Thanks a lot Ian, it's been a beautiful morning,' and Ian replied lightheartedly, 'We're not home yet.' A Chiang Mai bus was coming towards us on the opposite side of the road. We were just in the midst of passing it, and had nearly done so, when a big, strong, heavy vehicle, only a foot or two behind the bus that we were passing, suddenly shot out in front of us. He can have had no vision whatever of what was coming; he couldn't have seen us because he was so close behind the bus. Apparently they still haven't found the driver – he ran off. His vehicle must have been very strong for him not to have been injured more. There was another fellow sitting beside him who had his leg broken. The police know who he was. He had been seen drinking in Chainat that morning – usually that means 'strong drink', but we don't know, that's not official. There's so much bad driving in Thailand that it's possible.

One of the things that comforts me is that, when I saw that vehicle come out, my reaction was, 'There must be some way of avoiding this – it can't hit us.' There wasn't time to have terror or fear, there wasn't time to have dread, and I'm sure nobody in the back of the minibus can have known about it. They were all happily talking together, and Julia behind us hadn't seen anything coming. There was just a fraction of a second between seeing the vehicle and the crash. I have just a vague recollection of hearing the sound of the crash, and then – it may have only been half a minute later – I came to and saw the shocking state of things. It's a comfort to me that our loved ones would have gone out just as quickly as I did, but they didn't wake up to the terror and the horridness. It's a lovely thing that they went straight to the Lord and they didn't have to wake up in this life with what was left. There was peace on their faces, and some smiles; it's a lovely thing, and we praise the Lord that there wasn't suffering. The Lord ordered that accident in a lovely way. We can hardly think that it was lovely, but you imagine – there wasn't any child left without any parent, there wasn't a parent left without any children, and we praise the Lord that there weren't more people left terribly injured yet still alive, leaving the doctors at the hospital to have to decide who they were going to treat. We praise the Lord that the dear Gordon-Smiths and Sampsons went all together as families, and it's a comfort to Bryan and Adèle and me that our little ones and Twink went with those who were so dear to them.

Adèle Juzi had been reluctant to allow her two boys to go on the outing. Ulrich was doing a ward round and had taken their eldest boy, Daniel, with him, and she felt that he might be disappointed not to find the other two at home when he returned. But they pleaded, there was room for them, and so she gave her consent. After they had been gone some little while she began to have an intensely uneasy feeling about them. She paused in her work and committed them to the Lord. Ulrich returned with Daniel. The party was not back; the telephone rang, and Adèle *knew* before she answered it. She went out to the compound and saw the injured being brought in. She jumped in her car and drove out to the scene of the accident hoping there might be someone she could still help. She saw that the Lord had 'called the twelve unto himself',* her youngest son among them.

---

* These words from Matthew 10:1 refer, in their context of course, to the twelve disciples. As all who died in the accident were Christ's, and so went to be with him in heaven, the phrase naturally had a special poignancy.

Adèle recalls that moment: 'As I looked at the Thai people gathered round, my heart was filled with pity for them. I prayed, and turning to them I said, 'These people who have died are not here any more. They are already with the Lord, and they were ready to meet him. I have one wish – that you, all of you, will never forget this sad scene, and that whenever you hear anything about the Lord Jesus you will open your hearts to him, so that when you too have to die you will be as ready to meet the Lord as these people have been.'

How People Responded

In England John Townsend heard the news and immediately flew back to Thailand. Afterwards he said, 'Adèle's first words to me were, "God is good." Her face was that of Mary at the foot of the cross. And Ulrich? "The Lord gave and the Lord has taken away; blessed be the name of the Lord."'

The telephone rang in the home of Dr John Upsdell and his wife Alex, at Basildon in Essex. They had been at Manorom previously, but John was now doing a GP course at Basildon Hospital. Without hesitation they applied for permission to return, and with their two little girls, the younger only six weeks old, they went back to Manorom for six months, making a very valuable contribution to the work.

On this particular weekend John and Sue Belstead, surgeon and anaesthetist, were having to make one of the most important decisions of their lives. In a natural hiatus in John's career, should he engage in academic work for two years or volunteer for service overseas? They asked the Lord to show them. They heard on the radio the news of the accident, and they had the answer – God's call to

Manorom.

The lives of Dr Julia Brown with severe fractures, and Jonathan Juzi with internal haemorrhage, were only saved because a young man got off the bus and managed to persuade the driver of a passing vehicle to take the injured to hospital. A simple request, one might think, and so it would be in the West, but not so in Thailand where the belief is that if someone dies in your vehicle their spirit will haunt you.

This was to be, for Julia, the beginning of a long road back to recovery; a journey accomplished with such courage and faith that it has been an inspiration to know her in these days.

Apart from the two seriously injured, and now recovered, Rosemary herself had a broken arm, and there were minor injuries to Matthew Parry and Ben Farrington.

Bryan Parry operated to save the lives of the injured, with the knowledge that he had lost his wife and two little girls. The faith and peace which he displayed at this time, and in the months to follow, can only be described as 'passing all understanding', and is a privilege to record.

On the following Tuesday 17 January a crowd of some 700 people gathered in the compound of Manorom Hospital for a memorial and thanksgiving service. People had come in from the village, some of them having worked far into the night to make beautiful floral tributes in silk and cotton. Others left their work in the rice fields to share in the grief of those who had lost their friends and loved ones. The love of the Lord Jesus, the driving force behind these missionaries, was evidenced in the address given in English with Thai interpretation. Extracts from the Gospels, presented by the Scripture Gift Mission, were offered to all, and several hundred were accepted.

On the following day, Wednesday 18 January, a simple burial service was conducted in the Protestant cemetery in

Bangkok, and in a lovely peaceful spot down by the river they were laid to rest side by side in a communal grave. Those who had lost so much experienced the Lord's presence in such reality that, as Peter Farrington wrote, 'I could only praise him through my tears.' Months later, when Sir Fred Catherwood found himself seated at a dinner next to the British Ambassador's wife from Bangkok, she told him, 'I went to that funeral and felt such a reality about the faith of those bereaved. I have never in my life experienced anything like it. I was very deeply moved.'

As the news spread worldwide, hundreds of letters flowed in from near and far, expressing love and prayer. One friend wrote, 'There is nothing that we can say to you that the Lord will not have told you already.' How true! He was constantly reminding us of his promises, the first and most immediate one being, 'What I do thou knowest not now, but *thou shalt know* hereafter' – and we were held in his grip. There were also little human messages thoughtfully sent, and comforting:

From a relative: 'They have just caught an earlier train.'
From a church member: 'We don't understand – HE DOES!'
And from a young couple at our church:

Just think,
Of stepping on shore and finding it heaven,
Of taking hold of a hand and finding it God's hand,
Of breathing new air and finding it celestial air,
Of feeling invigorated and finding it immortality,
Of passing from storm and tempest and finding it unknown
   calm,
Of waking up and finding it home.

Many other letters came also reminding us of God's promises, on which we can rely, for, as Dr Michael Griffiths said at the thanksgiving service at All Souls Church in London, 'With God there are mysteries, *but no mistakes.*'

Grief

C.S. Lewis in his book *A Grief Observed* says, 'No one ever told me that grief felt so like fear.'

To that I would add that no one ever told me that heart-ache is a real physical pain in the centre of one's being that only time will ease. And no one ever told me that grief is like being trapped in a prison from which there is no escape.

No one told me, but I found out for myself, that as in the darkest moments one threw oneself upon the Lord, time and time again – and unfailingly – there would be the whisper, 'Peace, be still,' 'and there was a great calm'. I knew that God was real, that he was there, that he cared for me enough to entrust me with an experience such as this.

Stephanie

You grew in beauty through that last long year,
That bound you to this earth –
You walked with dignity, and joy, and hope,
Awaiting the new life that would not see
The sin and turmoil of our stricken world.

Your home became a place of peace and rest,
Where Ian could forget the frets and burdens of his
   busy life,
And others, too, would come to share
The fellowship of friends and family.

And so, as long as life shall last,
We'll keep the treasured memory of all your love
For Ian, Rachel, Mark
And still so much to spare for us
Who came – and went – and bore the darkest hour
And now await – the DAWN.

E.L. G-S

Epilogue

by Bryan Parry

We pass through an unkempt corner of Bangkok, walk along a gravel path in the overgrown cemetery, and arrive at 'our' quiet corner backing onto the mighty Chao Praya River, flowing silently and strongly alongside. Stephen and Sarah get to work busily arranging their market flowers by 'Becky' and 'Adèle' on the gravestone, sisters they have never met but, in the uncomplicated way of children, regard as real and theirs. Matthew, as older brother, is mediating in the dispute as to who should get the extra flower, 'Becky because she was older,' or, 'No, the baby should get one too.' Susan is silently sweeping off the leaves by Twink's name and placing orchids.

There is no awkwardness: love binds our old and new family naturally and inclusively. I feel awe. I tremble at the sheer magnitude of my loss; I marvel too at the mystery that without the accident I wouldn't love Susan or even have Stephen and Sarah. I affirm inwardly and silently beauty from ashes, oil of gladness for mourning, and a garment of praise for despair as I respond to a little voice saying, 'Another vase please, Daddy.'

Twenty years on and the legacy of Ian's life and the circumstances of his death retain their sharp poignancy. Understandably this is mainly for those who loved him and knew him best, including me. But many readers have been touched by his story through this remarkable little book which has turned up in surprising places, including the bedside lockers of my patients in New Zealand.

On one level it seems to be a tragic tale of the waste of a rare talent and promising life. Indeed, God appears both astonishingly unsentimental about his work and outrageously prodigal with his servants' lives and careers. The health and safety aspects of his job description for Christian discipleship seem decidedly deficient! Yet for those of us who went first-hand through this most unthinkable of events, which claimed not only Ian's life but eleven more of our loved ones, a different and compelling conclusion emerged.

Simply this: God can be trusted. Even through the indescribable unhinging and disequilibrium that comes from the pain and loss of family – he is there. The 'love of God' is no longer merely a theological formulation or trite, pious phrase but the bedrock of existence itself. The 'whys' and the 'what fors' of the uncomprehending mind become irrelevant in the shelter of his arms and the eerie sensation of his unbidden presence. He who is 'the resurrection and the life' has come to satisfy the human heart in its worst moment of deepest need. The 'treasures of darkness, riches stored in secret places' (Isaiah 43:3, NIV) are given gratuitously by a loving heavenly Father. Heaven itself seems separated by a mere membrane only microns thick. Realisation dawns that your loved ones are his loved ones and that they are alive. He can be trusted for them; he can be trusted to get you through. For the Manorom Hospital and wider OMF family in 1978, the result was a community of grieving, sharing and loving friends experiencing profound intimacy with

God and each other. I am different now; I no longer fear death.

Ian taught and influenced me profoundly. He is largely responsible for my post-Manorom direction of academic surgery, for example. But it was his infectious energy, enthusiasm and excellence in his Christian life that remain his most unforgettable contribution to me. Ian's life encourages us all to make the right response to God's teasing and provocative challenge in Isaiah 49:6 – 'It is too small a thing for you to be my servant to restore the tribes of Jacob and bring back those of Israel I have kept. I will also make you a light for the Gentiles, that you may bring my salvation to the ends of the earth.'

Auckland, January 1998

Bryan Parry continued working at Manorom until early 1982, apart from a period of training at St Mary's Hospital in London, where Ian had studied. He then returned to New Zealand for Matthew to start his secondary education. In God's providence, Bryan was soon to meet Susan Lea, a gastroenterologist, and they were married five months later in August 1982. She wrote in a letter to a friend around that time, 'Matthew makes our joy complete.' In 1985 their son Stephen was born, and Sarah followed in 1989.

Bryan is now Professor and Head of Surgery in the School of Medicine and Health Science at the University of Auckland, and Chief of Surgical Services, Auckland Hospital.

A letter from Peter Farrington, dental surgeon, and his wife Rosemary, a nurse

The Christian Hospital

Manorom
Thailand

February 1978

Dear Friends who have shared and sorrowed with us.

This verse has become very dear to us: 'He called unto him the twelve that they might be with him.' One of the twelve was our precious little boy, Johnny, just five years old. We love our Johnny (we're glad not to have to put it in the past tense) and the thought of the Lord's delighting in him, a perfect little boy in Jesus' robe of righteousness, and of Johnny thrilling in the presence of the Lord Jesus is very precious to us.

The evening before the accident, at his Bible story time, Johnny asked me, 'Mummy, what will it be like in heaven?' I showed him the diamonds in my ring and tried to explain what I understood of the beauties of heaven, telling him there was no sun there – that God was the light of heaven. He asked, 'Mummy, what will we wear?' and

I told him, 'Beautiful clothes, white and shining.' He was very excited. The story that evening was of Jacob's death in Egypt and of his sons taking his body back for burial in Canaan. He asked, 'What would they put a body in?' and I replied, 'There are special boxes to put bodies in.' 'Are there little ones for little children too?' Johnny asked me. Johnny's little body is in a little box in one long grave right in the middle, between dear little friends, and at each end the 'Aunties and Uncles' that he loved so much.

They all died instantly, feeling no pain, going for ever to be with the Lord, and we believe that that Saturday was a very precious day in heaven. As we look back to the accident and all the events surrounding it, we can do nothing but praise the Lord for his goodness and his mercy.

I was sitting in the front passenger seat nursing Ben. The impact caused the door to fly off, allowing us to be thrown out. Although the vehicle that pulled out in front of us was only about two metres away, it just gave me time to tighten my grip on Ben and we were hurled out together. I came to shortly afterwards, to see bodies all around me.

Contrary to the usual Thai action, a dear young Thai man got off a bus and tried to stop vehicles passing to take the five of us surviving to hospital. People are loath to help for fear of evil spirits if somebody should die in their vehicle. Time was precious because of the serious condition of two people, and although a number of cars were unwilling to give aid, miraculously two acquaintances of the Thai man came by in a Land Rover and he lifted us in. How we praise the Lord for the provision of this young man, Soomet. Please pray for him.

As to our testimony, I always knew that the Lord loved me, but these last two weeks he has poured his love down in a way I never knew would be possible. I've often tried to face the thought of what my reaction would be should the Lord take one of my children, having heard of women who had glorified the Lord in such tragedy. I knew that I was one who could not. We've cried many tears for Johnny and we can't help but miss him, but it's with no pious pretence that I can say I'm happy, happy, happy that our little one has gone on to his reward. God in his grace has opened my mouth to be able to witness for him in a way that I never knew before. This, in itself, has been like ointment on the wound.

* * *

As for me, Peter, on Saturday morning 14 January, I said goodbye to my family and went to Paknampho with others from Manorom Church to help in visitation of houses in preparation for the coming Church Growth Campaign in March.

At 2.15 pm I was told by Geoff Case and Mr Yod, the head carpenter from Manorom Hospital, that the Manorom minibus had been in a serious accident and that Rosemary and the children were involved. Immediately we set off to return to Manorom with Peter Draper, Deputy Superintendent, not knowing what we would find on arrival at the hospital. On the way Mr Yod gave us more details, and the Lord graciously poured his peace into my heart so that I could trust him. We passed the scene of the accident and saw our hospital vehicle completely crushed by a large van. I said to Peter Draper, 'Nobody could have survived that accident.' And a policeman at the scene told me they had taken twelve bodies to Manorom. As we came into the hospital I was so conscious of a tremendous peace and assurance that God, our Saviour, was in control. I found Ben in the Emergency Room waiting for surgery, Rosemary in the ward, and was told that our darling Johnny was already in the Lord's presence in glory.

Bryan Parry, the surgeon on duty, although numbed by the loss of his dear wife, Twink, and two little girls, was able to operate on Jonathan Juzi, who had internal injuries. He also stitched up his own son, Matthew's foot. Then I attended to Ben's cut head and face, and was so thankful that the Lord helped me to be a surgeon and not a father for that operation. Dr June Morgan operated on Rosemary, and then Bryan and I operated on Dr Julia Brown. The Lord poured his strength into us at that time and we praise him for all that he enabled us and all the staff to do that day and in the days following. The fellowship and concern so evident here among missionary and Thai staff has been wonderful, and we pray, 'Long may it continue!'

Manorom, which is known as a very hard place in its reaction to the gospel message, has softened in a way that is hardly believable. At a memorial service on the Tuesday after the accident, hundreds of market people and government officials sat and listened intently to the message of hope. The schools were officially closed so that teachers could attend if they wished.

You will realise that we haven't overcome the grief that there will still be. Please don't stop praying for us in the months ahead, Especially pray for Bryan Parry, who will soon leave his only remaining child, seven-year-old Matthew, at school in Chefoo, and be returning alone to Manorom.

In his love,

Peter, Rosemary and Ben

3 February 1978. Rosemary left hospital yesterday. Her

broken arm, ribs, injured eye and lacerations are healing, but she is emotionally very tired. Ben has quite recovered and is happy to have his Mummy home. Please continue to pray.

Address given by Dr Michael Griffiths at the Memorial Service in All Souls Church, London, on 28 February 1978

'Brace yourself like a man.' Do you recognise the context of these words? They are found in the Book of Job, where in the opening chapter we read of disaster striking a family: 'While he was still speaking, yet another messenger came and said, "Your sons and your daughters were feasting and drinking wine in the eldest brother's house, when suddenly a mighty wind swept in from the desert and struck the four corners of the house. It collapsed on them and they are dead, and I am the only one who has escaped to tell you!"' (Job 1:18).

After many chapters arguing about unexplained suffering, Job is confronted by God himself: 'The Lord answered Job out of the storm. He said: 'Who is this that darkens my counsel with words without knowledge? Brace yourself like a man; I will question you, and you shall answer me' (Job 38:1–2).

It was a desert storm which had destroyed Job's family. And it is 'out of the storm' that the Lord answers Job. One of the most moving things in the book is Job's reaction. He tore his clothes, shaved his head, fell to the ground, and he worshipped. He said, 'Naked I came from my mother's womb, and naked I shall depart. The Lord gave and the Lord has taken away; may the name of the Lord be praised' (Job 1:21). The writer tells us that in all his suffering, Job did not sin, nor did he blame God. But throughout this book we find Job and his friends asking human questions and suggesting human answers, as surely we have done. As we have heard what happened on the road to Manorom, let's be honest. Let's not pretend that we as Christians have no questions. Indeed, we might have fewer questions if we were not Christians, if we did not believe in a faithful God who cares.

People drive carelessly, people drive without responsibility, and nobody is immune from the suffering that results from this. All of us who drive know that. But because we do believe in a loving God, we wonder why on earth he didn't choose to intervene. Why didn't he intervene on this occasion in order to rescue these committed servants of his who had sacrificed so much to serve in rural Thailand?

We cannot escape the problem by blaming it glibly on the enemy, of whom Christ spoke. When weeds were found mixed with the wheat, you remember, Christ said, 'An enemy did this' (Mt 13:28). He taught that when the words of the gospel are preached, there is an enemy who snatches the seed away (Mt 13:19). This happens for us when we have decided to think about Christ, to pause for a moment in our headlong rush, to ask ourselves what we're living for, where we're going. We mean to think about it, we mean to stop, and yet somehow we never get round to it. There is an enemy who snatches away the seed. There is an enemy who lays snares for Christians, and if they fall into them, makes certain that it gets into the newspapers. Should we blame the devil for this accident? Perhaps. C.S. Lewis wrote powerfully about the activity of the devil and his minions in *The Screwtape*

Letters. Here is an enemy who hinders churches, who tries to stop missionary work. So is it the enemy's hand that we see here, active as we know it was in the Book of Job?

But still we cannot escape the problem of why God allows such tragedies to happen. Why did he permit this one? These are real questions. Why is God so wasteful with his resources? So prodigal in spending lives that have been given to him? These were gifted young men and women in their prime, giving their golden years to serve Christ in missionary service. Why waste their lives? Now that question isn't a new one either – you'll find that in the Bible too. 'Why this waste?' people asked, when an expensive box of perfume was broken and its fragrance poured over the head of Jesus on his way to the cross. '[It] could have been sold and the money given to the poor!' (Mt 26:6–13).

The following poem was sent to Peter and Rosemary Farrington, who lost their son, Johnny. It's called 'Psalm on the Death of an Eighteen-year-old Son', and was written by Joe Bayley who had already lost his two younger sons. This is what he wrote expressing his pain at the loss of the third in all the honesty of his heart:

> What waste, Lord
> this ointment precious
> here outpoured
> is treasure great
> beyond my mind to think.
> For years
> until this midnight,
> it was safe contained
> awaiting careful use
> now broken
> wasted
> lost.
> The world is poor
> so poor it needs each drop

of such a store.
This treasure spent
might feed a multitude
for all their days
and then yield more.
This world is poor?
It's poorer now
the treasure's lost.
I breathe its lingering fragrance
soon even that
will cease.
What purpose served?
The act is void of reason
sense
Lord
madmen do such deeds
not sane.
The sane man hoards his treasure
spends with care
if good
to feed the poor
or else to feed himself.
Let me alone Lord.
You've taken from me
what I'd give your world.
I cannot see
such waste
that you should take what poor men need.
You have a heaven
full of treasure
could you not wait to exercise your claim
on this? O spare me Lord forgive
that I may see
beyond this world
beyond myself
your sovereign plan
or seeing not may trust you
spoiler of my treasure.

Have mercy, Lord.
Here is my quit claim.[1]

Of course we have questions! Why is the Lord apparently so unkind to his friends, who serve him, who've given up so much to follow him? We must not pretend that we have no questions. Nor that we have all the answers. Still less can we take refuge in clichés. The Bible says a lot about suffering. The Bible centres upon the suffering of God, on the Son of God, who comes into this world in order to give his life a ransom for us, and who died that we might be forgiven. And that's the core of it all. He tells us, as we saw in our reading, that the seed must fall into the ground and die, and then it will bring forth fruit. If we hang on to life, if we fear to risk it, we lose it. If we're ready to hazard it, we gain it. It's in that context that he says, 'Whoever serves me must follow me' (Jn 12:24–26). The whole orientation of the Bible seems to swing on this pivot of the suffering of God in Christ. In the Old Testament, suffering is a problem: 'Why do the righteous suffer?' asks Job. 'Why do the wicked not suffer?' asks the Psalmist in Psalm 73.

But in the New Testament everything is turned round. Christians must expect to suffer. Suffering is no longer a problem – it becomes a privilege! Thus Paul says to young Christians in Thessalonica, that he's writing so that no one may be led astray by these afflictions: 'When we were with you, we kept telling you that we would be persecuted. And it turned out that way, as you well know' (1 Thess 3:4). New converts were warned of difficulty for those entering the kingdom of heaven (Acts 14:22). Jesus told his disciples: '[Congratulations] when people insult you, persecute you, and falsely say all kinds of evil against you because of me. Rejoice . . . for in the same way they persecuted the prophets who were before you' (Mt 5:11).

We cannot escape the fact that the Christian symbol is

the cross – that Christ has suffered and that those who follow him must expect to share in some measure of suffering just because they do follow him. And as I meet each generation of new missionaries coming through Singapore for orientation, and play volleyball with people like Noel Sampson, I can't help being reminded again and again that the missionary life is no picnic. We're there in Asia because the work that we do is a matter of life and death. Because it really matters whether people go as missionaries or not. And so Paul writing to the Colossians says, 'I rejoice in what was suffered for you, and I fill up in my flesh what is still lacking in regard to Christ's afflictions, for the sake of his body, which is the church' (Col 1:24).

If there had never been men and women who were ready to follow Christ in suffering, the Church would never have been planted at all in countries like Thailand. One hundred and fifty years ago, in 1828, Gutzlaff and Tomlin made their home in the grounds of the Portuguese Embassy in Bangkok. Carl Gutzlaff (1803–51) travelled to Singapore on three weeks leave, where he met Maria Newell of the London Missionary Society in Malacca. He met her, courted her and married her in 1829 – all in his three weeks leave! And he took her back with him to Bangkok. He was a fast worker, Gutzlaff. But you had to be in those days. The two of them worked together on the translation of the New Testament. Soon she was expecting children – twin babies. They were born, and she died, within a year of their marriage. Within eighteen months, both Tomlin and Gutzlaff had left Bangkok in serious ill health.

Those early missionaries died like flies, in the heat, in their long, unhealthy western garments. Few of them ever expected to return home; very few of them ever did. It was a world without any protective innoculations against

typhoid or cholera. There were no antibiotics and no pro-
phylactics against malaria until after World War Two –
that explains just why Manorom is there in central
Thailand! It's an area where no foreign missionaries had
been able to live because of endemic cerebral malaria that
every year killed tens of thousands of Thai people. Few of
the first pioneers lived more than two or three years – not
long enough to learn the language well enough, not long
enough to be able to explain the gospel clearly enough, in
the Thai language, to people with a Buddhist background. No wonder that it took nineteen years before missionaries to Thailand saw the first persons converted –
and they were Chinese and not Thai.

One of the significant medical pioneers, later on, was
Dr Samuel House (1817–76), who was the first in Thailand
(and possibly in East Asia) to vaccinate against smallpox
and to operate with anaesthetics. Medical missionaries
have always been in the forefront. The first resident
Christian in Korea was a doctor. Hudson Taylor of the
China Inland Mission was medically trained. Today in
Nepal, in Afghanistan, in the Yemen, in Bhutan, Christian
doctors are at the forefront of Christian witness. Travel
has always been dangerous in Thailand. Dr House was
seriously injured on two occasions: once he was thrown
from his horse, and once he was gored by an elephant
when crossing the swampy areas of central Thailand of
those days.[2] So this most recent accident is one of a chain
of accidents and deaths among missionaries in Thailand.
We in OMF lost two nurses taken for ransom and killed
two years ago, and two Swiss men in northern Thailand
were murdered last year, all for Jesus, who suffered for us
and calls us to follow: 'Whoever serves me must follow
me.'

The Christian not only suffers and shares in the suffering of God to save the world, but he also submits to the

sovereignty of God. This is not the submission of the weak to the strong, or the small to the great: that is submission through fear. That's the kind of fatalism from which we come to preach deliverance. Submission is not even that of the sinful to the holy. Thai people believe that suffering is the result of sin: that was one of the answers in the Book of Job that was rejected, you remember. It is rather the submission of faith to the one who loves us. Paul's longing for himself and for his Christian converts was that Christ may be magnified in our bodies, whether by our living or by our dying (Phil 1:20). Paul first became a Christian because he saw Christ glorified in the dying of Stephen. Already the mother of one of the injured doctors has become a Christian, led to Christ through the father of Twink Parry. The wonder of what God does, and the attitude of bereaved relatives has been a testimony to this. It has carried the certainty that God is a God who loves and cares.

I sent a different poem to Bryan Parry, the New Zealand surgeon. Here's a man who scrubbed up and operated on the survivors when his own heart was breaking, knowing that the bodies of his own wife, of his unborn child, and of his two daughters were in the wreck. He's there, serving others with a breaking heart, left to look after his own six-year-old son, Matthew. And I sent him this:

> I am hurt, Lord,
> I don't want courage, or a blithe spirit,
> Or faith, or hope or charity,
> I don't want to fight or even stand and
> turn the other cheek to fate,
> I want to run, to cringe first –
> then run and hide myself at the back
> gate of hell, despairing,
> flatly wrinkled like a pricked balloon.
>
> I am hurt, Lord,
> Don't quote holy writs to me,

Don't even say, 'Lo I am with you',
I know all that, and
it doesn't matter for the moment.
Just hold me, Lord,
Tight-fisted, with a grip like
all eternity.
You do it,
I can't hold on,
Not even with one finger.
I for whom some others run
for counsel, and the handclasp of
faith and hope and charity.
Hold on, Lord,
It will pass.
But for the moment,
Hold.[3]

That is the submission of faith. There's no comfort in clichés. Only in God. I may not be able to hold on to God, but God can hold on to me. A real God, whom I love whether I live or die. That's what Job found, and he submitted his own questionings and lack of answers. 'Brace yourself like a man.' And from that braced man, Bryan, I got a letter back. At the bottom he added a verse: 'They shall not labour in vain, or bear children for calamity; for they shall be the offspring of the blessed of the Lord, and their children with them' (Is 65:23, RSV). Let me read from the letter:

Certainly these are days of grief and weeping, but certainly not days of regret. Francis Schaeffer used to be fond of challenging people with, 'Is your position big enough to cover all of life?' and then point out that only Christianity has all the big answers. The Lord has proved himself to be more than sufficient to my need. His loving attention to all the details has touched me too. Matthew is proving strong spiritually and emotionally. He has vivid memories of the accident, but is able to talk it all out in my arms. We have wept together too.

Let's put it this way: It's not that the foolish unbeliever builds on the sand and the wind blows and the rain comes and the floods beat on his insubstantial foundations, and the wise man builds his house on the rock and the sun shines all day long. Not at all. The wise believer suffers the same storms, the same winds and rains and floods as does the unbelieving man. But because of his faith in God, his rock, the house of his life stands. Is your position big enough to cover all of life? Bryan's is.

But it's not only the suffering of God in which Christians are called to share. Nor just the sovereignty of God to which Christians submit in quiet confidence. But rather it is the salvation of God to which Christians look forward and of which Christians speak. The word 'salvation' sounds like Christian jargon, so let's call it God's great salvage operation. I think it's very easy for some of us to get wrong ideas about what 'good news' means to Christians. It's not just posthumous benefits, individual survival after death, that might be no more than 'pie in the sky when you die'. Let's be clear, that is a part of the gospel. And this evening don't we rejoice in that part of it? Aren't we glad that that is true? That there is, as we were reminded this evening, a place 'reserved in heaven for you' (1 Pet 1:4).

But it's also for this life too. It's the quality of living with God, and for God, and belonging to him, and enjoying the integration of life and meaning which he gives. It's the blessing which he gives to families who love and trust him, like the Sampsons and the Gordon-Smiths, and the Parrys, and the Farringtons and the Juzis. It's not just waiting until we die to reap posthumous benefits. That's real also, isn't it?

Let me illustrate from their own situation in Thailand. Think of leprosy patients. A Malay, a former Muslim in southern Thailand, testified at the funeral of those murdered nurses, what it meant to have them take his ulcerated leprous feet upon their knees and bathe and bind them up. He saw the love of Christ in that. Our missionary medical team nowadays can treat leprosy. Surgeons do tendon transplant operations to help them gain use of their hands and feet. Then the physiotherapists come along to help them practise using them, and the occupational therapists teach them skills with their hands so that they can engage in remunerative work and regain their self-respect. But there's something else that Christian doctors and nurses do. Tell them, as the Bible says, that he, Jesus, the Lord and Saviour who is coming, he will refashion the bodies of our humiliation to be like his glorious body. That body which medics can patch up for a few more years, God will totally remake and refashion. Isn't that what we confess in the creed when we say, 'I believe in the forgiveness of sins, in the resurrection of the body'? Leprosy patients love that truth when medical missionaries make time to explain it to them.

Do you know what Thai people believe? They love their families as we do. But when their loved ones die, they believe they become *phi*, that is they become hostile spirits to be afraid of. They really do need the good news of the gospel. That good news of Christ promises a new body in heaven. The Japanese poet, Kobayashi Issa, a Buddhist, lost his one surviving son, and his Buddhist comforters gathered round him like some Buddhist Job. They tried to comfort him, and this is what they said, 'This is a world of illusion, a world of dew. It's not real. Your child was an illusion. You imagined him. And you are an illusion too. There's nothing you can do about it.' *Shikata ga nai* (literally: 'there is no way') as we express fatalistic resignation to our fate in Japan. Issa replied, with a seventeen-syllable poem, which translates like this: 'The world of dew is a world of dew – and yet – and yet.'

The human heart, Buddhist, Hindu or agnostic, longs for reality; we long that those whom we love may have real existence, and that when they die, as die they will, that we may meet them again. Christians have something important to say about this. For Paul writes: 'We believe that Jesus died and rose again and so we believe that God will bring with Jesus those who have fallen asleep in him' (1 Thess 4:14). The Christian missionary has a message to declare in Thailand. Those coffins laid out there in Bangkok: the people that we knew and appreciated are not there any more. Their broken bodies were there – discarded like empty gloves, when hands have been pulled out of them and need them no more. We sorrow and grieve for losing those we love, but they are not lost in sorrow, but found in Christ. Why were those doctors there in Thailand? Just to meet medical need? There are, after all, good government hospitals nearby. Why were they there in the never-ending heat of the flat, humid Thailand plain? Because of God's salvation, to be offered to people who need it and who rejoice in it when they find it, but don't know they need it until they do find it.

In a Christian land, the ethics of the Good Samaritan are taken for granted, even by people who are not committed to the Jesus who told us the parable of the Good Samaritan. Have a road accident here and people run to help. What happened in this accident? Here's the crashed vehicle, twelve dead, five still breathing. People are running all right, but to search the bodies, to rob the pockets of the dead and of the living. To steal cameras. Does that shock you? That's why they're there. That's why we go out as missionaries, to change all that – because people are in spiritual darkness and because they need the love of Jesus to forgive them, and the teaching of Jesus to change them, and the power of the spirit of Jesus to enable us all to do what we know to be right. There was in the end a Thai Good Samaritan, who came and stopped a truck to get the injured to hospital. Significantly, he was someone who had already been in touch with the Christian hospital and the missionaries who worked there.

There is a spiritual need as well as a medical need. And these missionaries, these families we remember with thanksgiving tonight, were and are committed to serving Jesus Christ, whatever the cost. What are you committed to? What are you spending your life doing? Is your position big enough to cover all of life? Ian was so right when he said, 'Don't make special things of missionaries.' It's not the stuff that missionaries are made of that matters – it's the God who is their maker, and who can make us too. So as we conclude tonight, what response do we make as we consider the challenge of the lives we give thanks for? We thank him for making them into what they became. Will we let him make of us what he wants to make of us? And what of Thailand? These families had a deep love for this land of green rice and running water, with its fruits and fish and brilliant birds. And they had a deep longing for its people in their human need – both medically and spiritually – to bring bodily healing for the remainder of their human lifespan, and healing for the human heart which lasts for ever. They gave their lives because they longed that needy, impoverished, hungry people might find life in Christ.

Notes

1 Joe Bayley, *Psalms of My Life* (Coverdale House Publishers: Illinois, 1969).
2 Kenneth Wells, *History of Protestant Work in Thailand 1828–1858* (CCT: Bangkok, 1958); Donald Lord, *Mo Bradley and Thailand* (Eerdmans: Grand Rapids, 1969).
3 Sally Chambers, American poet.

English-speaking OMF Centres

OMF
Station Approach
Borough Green
Sevenoaks
Kent TN15 8BG
UK

OMF
PO Box 849
Epping
NSW 2121
AUSTRALIA

OMF
5759 Coopers Avenue
Mississauga ON
L4Z 1R9
CANADA

OMF
2 Cluny Road
Singapore 259570
REPUBLIC OF SINGAPORE

OMF
PO Box 10–159
Balmoral
Auckland 1
NEW ZEALAND

OMF
10 West Dry Creek Circle
Littleton
CO 80120-4413
USA

OMF
PO Box 3080
Pinegowrie 2123
SOUTH AFRICA

Precious to God
Sarah Bowen   £5.99 in UK

Two young people, delighted to be starting a family, have their expectations shattered by the arrival of a handicapped child. And yet this is only the first of many difficulties to be faced. What was initially a tragedy, is through faith, transformed into a story of inspiration, hope and spiritual enrichment.

'I was deeply moved by Sarah's story. Do read it.'
Celia Bowring

Angels Keep Watch
Carol Hathorne   £5.99 in UK

A true adventure showing how God still directs our lives, not with wind, earthquake or fire, but by the still small voice.

'Go to Africa.' The Lord had been saying it for over forty years. At last, Carol Hathorne had obeyed, going out to Kenya with her husband. On the eastern side of Nairobi, where tourists never go, they came face to face with dangers, hardship and poverty on a daily basis, but experienced the joy of learning that Christianity is still growing in God's world.

Carol Hathorne is an Anglican priest working in a parish near Dudley, West Midlands. Her husband, Mark, is a Methodist minister in the same area.

God's Catalyst
Rosemary Green   £8.99 in UK

The highly commended guide to prayer counselling.

Rosemary Green's international counselling ministry has prayer and listening to God at it's heart. Changed lives and rekindled faith testify to God's healing power. Here she provides insight, inspiration and advice for both counsellors and concerned lay Christians who long to be channels of God's Spirit to help those in need.

God's Catalyst is a unique tool for the non-specialist counsellor; for the pastor who has no training; for the lay Christian who wants to come alongside hurting friends.

'To read this book will be helpful to any Christian interested in helping others.'

John White

Women Celebrating Faith
Lucinda S. McDowell   £5.99 in UK

In this challenging and gripping collection, women from all walks of life take time to look back on their lives at forty and reflect on the spiritual lessons they've learned. No matter what your age you will be encouraged by the experiences of these women.

'A book that makes you look forward to mid-life.'

Susan Yates